Why Just Cook It?

Make It Fool Proof

Recipes for professional results with the shake of a jar!

Mark Coulton Pierce

In Great Taste Publishing
Dallas, Texas

Published by: In Great Taste Publishing
              P.O.Box 225225
              Dallas, Texas   75222-5225

Manufactured in the United States of America

Designed by Aardvark Advertising
Covers by Covington Photography
In conjunction with Fool Proof Gourmet Products®

First Edition 1999

Dedication

To my wife, Teryl, who told me I could do it.

To my mother, Roseann, who told me that if I wanted Banana Pudding I had to make the meringue and then handed me two forks!

To my father, Wilson, who told me that if you are to be the best, you have to eat it, drink it and sleep it.

To Lloyd who showed me he believed.

And to Big Jack who always told me it tasted great!

About the Author

From the time Mark Coulton Pierce told his Marine Corps dad that he wanted to be a chef, he has worked to be the best, working for almost a decade in New Orleans' finest restaurants learning from some of the world's best chefs. Mark took that expertise on the road culminating in a stint as the Executive Chef at MGM Studios where he truly was "Chef to the Stars". It was while he was there that he developed the Fool Proof Gourmet Products line of seasoning blends so he could meet a chef's greatest challenge, which is that every plate that left his kitchen would taste as though Mark had prepared it himself. Professionally his seasoning blends were a hit. Meanwhile he married into a family who was culinarily challenged, to put it very kindly. Mark joked that dinner time was like the shoot out at the O K Corral, with each member of the family out waiting the other in the battle to see who would give in and cook a meal. Mark says he created his seasonings to assure quality in his restaurants. I believe it was really so he could get a good meal at home that he didn't have to cook himself, because even I (his wife) and his in-laws can and will cook a great meal with the shake of one jar.

Acknowledgements

Maybe not original but so true: "When the going gets tough the tough get going". Developing a new product line and getting it to your table was tough. But what I wanted was so simple. I wanted families to have fun fooling around in the kitchen, like mine did. I wanted to share home cooked meals that taste fantastic, even when I couldn't be there to cook them. I wanted everyone to say "yummo and thanks" to the cook. I wanted mealtime to be the best part of the day. And I did it. Even better, I found a way to put it in a jar so you can do it too! This is my gift to you.

And now is my opportunity to say thanks to those who helped me keep going:

To my wife Teryl for her love, help, encouragement, and support. You are my success in spite of myself.

Sherlock had his Watson, Caruso his Man Friday. Jeff Covington has been there for me since Fool Proof's infancy. His creative talents, help and friendship have been indispensable.

To the chefs who gave me the encouragement and support from the beginning, a big high five. Tom Valentin, Bernhard Muller, Ty Thoren, Didier Busnot, Kevin Graham, Greg Provine and Donald Perkins, you saw the quality and value of Fool Proof. Thank you for your honesty and patronage.

To Brian Shernak who opened the door and to Mike Richard who beat the streets, I can't thank you enough but this will have to do for now.

To Lloyd for his positive thinking and Marjorie for her culinary inspirations.

To my brothers and sisters for their old fashioned encouragement.

To Shane DeRolf, thanks for finding my glasses.

To Bruce and Erin Bell, a wing up for all of your help.

To Gael, who pushed all the right buttons.

To you all, a fool hearty thanks from the bottom of my jar.

Mark Coulton Pierce
The Foolish Gourmet®

Table of Contents

Appetizers

Soups, Salads, Sandwiches

Entrees, Sides and More

Beef

Poultry

Make It Fool Proof

Table of Contents

Fool Proof Baby Back Ribs

4 racks of baby back pork ribs
4 TB All Purpose Taste Massage

- ❑ To make ribs more tender ask the butcher to remove the membrane from the back of the ribs.
- ❑ Rub 1 TB All Purpose Taste Massage on each rack. Cover and let stand in refrigerator 4 to 6 hours for best flavor.
- ❑ Grill ribs on a hot grill for 4-5 minutes on each side to sear. Place ribs with curved side up over a low flame and continue cooking for 3-4 hours, basting every 20 minutes with the Fool Proof Baster. Baste both sides of rack returning it to curve side up position to continue cooking. *The ribs are done when the meat has pulled away exposing 1/4" to 3/8" of the bone. This is key because it's easy to cook ribs too long or too short a time causing them to be dry or tough.*
- ❑ Just before pulling ribs off the grill, brush with your favorite BBQ sauce or Rodeo Q (p.41). Leave on grill another minute just to warm sauce.

Slick E-Z Version: Sear on grill as above, then place ribs on a baking sheet curve side up in 300° oven for 3 hours basting both sides continuously with the Fool Proof Baster. Brush with BBQ sauce last minute.

Fool Proof Baster

1 C lt. brown sugar
1 C red wine vinegar
2 TB olive oil
1 TB Worcestershire Sauce
1/4 C dry sherry
1 tsp All Purpose Taste Massage

- ❑ Mix ingredients thoroughly in bowl. Use to baste any grilled item for a great open pit flavor.

Sister Sarah's Santa Fe Chicken Wings

2 lb chicken drummettes or segmented wings
2 TB + 1 tsp Santa Fe Sunset Blend

❑ Preheat oven to 450° and heat a skillet on stovetop on medium-high heat.
❑ In a large bowl toss chicken wings in 2 TB Santa Fe.
❑ Sprinkle hot skillet with 1 tsp Santa Fe, place seasoned wings in seasoned skillet, turning to sear all around, almost to the point of being blackened.
❑ Place skillet of wings in a 450° oven for 20 minutes for a great tasting *non-fried* chicken wings.

Slick E-Z Version: slightly different flavor than above but equally great taste!
❑ Preheat oven to 500°
❑ In a large bowl toss wings in Santa Fe at a rate of 1 TB per pound of chicken.
❑ Place on a cookie sheet in a single layer, skin side up.
❑ Bake at 500° for 30 minutes.

Pueblo Dipping Sauce

1 C bleu cheese dressing
2 tsp Santa Fe Sunset Blend
2 TB picante sauce
12 carrot sticks
12 celery sticks

❑ Combine bleu cheese dressing, Santa Fe and picante sauce. Mix well.
❑ Garnish dip bowl with carrot and celery sticks.

Sarah Pierce
Simpsonville, S. C.

Gingered Sates of Beef & Pork with Spicy Tai Peanut Sauce

1 lb sirloin steak (sliced ¼ " thin, slightly pounded)
1 lb pork loin (sliced ¼" thin, slightly pounded)
1 TB Steak & Burger Rubdown
wooden skewers (soaked in water)

❑ Slice and pound steak and pork then slice pounded portions in half lengthwise. Skewer meats and place beef and pork in separate shallow pans. Set aside. *Steak & Burger Rubdown will be applied after marinating.*

1/4 C soy sauce
1 TB ginger (fresh, grated)
2 TB peanut oil
1/4 tsp sesame oil
2 TB rice vinegar
1 TB ketchup
1 TB lt. brown sugar
2 cloves garlic (minced)
2 TB dry sherry
1 lemon (juice and zest)

❑ Combine ingredients in large mixing bowls. Pour marinade over skewered meats, let stand, covered in refrigerator for 1 hour.
❑ Preheat grill to very hot. Remove skewers from marinade, sprinkling each skewer with Steak & Burger.
❑ Place on grill cooking approximately 2 minutes each side.
❑ Serve with Spicy Tai Peanut Sauce.

FOOLISH NOTE: This ginger marinade is a great marinade for *any* grilled item.

Spicy Tai Peanut Sauce

1/4 C peanut butter
3 TB soy sauce
1 tsp ginger (fresh, grated)
3 TB ketchup
3 TB rice vinegar
1/4 C lt. brown sugar
1/2 tsp Steak & Burger Rubdown
1/4 tsp red pepper flakes
1 clove garlic (minced)
3 TB sherry
1/4 tsp sesame oil
3 TB Coco Lopez
2 TB pineapple juice

❑ Combine all ingredients in a microwavable bowl.
❑ Cook in microwave for 4 minutes stirring 4 times to incorporate well.

Mateo's Jalapeño Cream Mojo

1 lb sour cream
2 TB Santa Fe Sunset Blend
2 TB pickled jalapeños (minced)
2 TB pickled jalapeño juice
2 TB green onion (finely minced)
1 tsp cilantro (chopped) optional

❑ Thoroughly whisk together all *but* green onion and cilantro.
❑ Microwave for 3 minutes stirring 3 times.
❑ Add green onion and cilantro. Blend well. Refrigerate to chill.

Matt Pierce
Matt Daddy's Hunt & Fish Camp
Clarkston, Mi.

Appetizers

Cocktail Meatballs

2 lb ground beef (lean)
1/2 C onion (minced)
1/2 C green bell pepper (minced)
2 TB + 1 tsp All Purpose Taste Massage
3 egg yolks
1 whole egg
1/4 C ketchup
2 TB mustard (spicy brown is best)
2 tsp soy sauce
1 C white bread crumbs (fresh)
2 tsp steak sauce (your favorite)

- ❑ Preheat oven to 400°
- ❑ Combine ingredients in large bowl mixing thoroughly. Use your hands. Roll into meatballs. *Big time kid fun!*
- ❑ Place on cookie sheet, touching.
- ❑ Cook in 400° oven for 12-15 minutes for 1 oz. size meatball (cocktail size) or 15-20 minutes for 2 oz. meatball (spaghetti & meatball size)

THE FOOL SUGGESTS: Serve with Sauce Dauphine for dipping or topped with Tomato Marsala (p.30) for a fantastic meatball submarine sandwich!

All Purpose Taste Massage is a well-rounded and balanced taste seasoning that enhances rather than changes the natural flavor of foods. Rub on ribeye, flank steak, ribs and chicken. Good in tuna salad, roasted or stir fry vegetables, and spaghetti.

Santa Fe Sunset Blend has the wonderful flavor of Tabasco and jalapeño without the bitterness or high heat. Rub on sirloin strip, broil, top with favorite brown gravy or salsa. Makes quick as a shake fajita meat. Great on roasts, chicken or chops.

Sauce Dauphine

1 (1.2 oz)package Knorr Demi Glace *or* brown gravy mix
1 TB onion (minced)
1/2 C port wine
3/4 C water
2 TB current or red plum jelly
6 mushrooms (sliced & sautéed)
1/2 tsp All Purpose Taste Massage
1/8 tsp nutmeg (ground fresh if possible)
1 TB prepared mustard
2 TB sour cream

❑ Combine ingredients *except mustard and sour cream* in microwavable bowl, mixing well.
❑ Cook in microwave on high setting for 6 minutes, stirring 3 times during the cooking process.
❑ Add mustard and sour cream. Blend well.
❑ Microwave an additional minute being sure not to boil sauce again which would make sour cream curdle and mustard bitter.

THE FOOL SUGGESTS: This sauce is great for open faced roast beef sandwiches or pork chops.

Steak & Burger Rubdown gives you Five Star Steak House flavor at home. Mix it at a rate of 1 TB per pound of ground beef, another shake on top of patty for the *best* hamburger! Enjoy it in a seasoned flour for chicken fried steaks and the like.

Seafood Serenade is a citrus blend of spices with a velvety buttery taste. Apply liberally for blackened, broiled or baked seafood recipes. Use with white wine for fabulous poaching liquor. Rub on chicken for lemon chicken flavor. Mix 1 TB per 1 cup of flour or cornmeal for sautéing or frying.

Matt Daddy's Sauté Shrimp Cocktail

2 lbs shrimp (peeled) 35 count shrimp are The Fool's favorite
2 TB + 1 tsp Seafood Serenade
2 TB canola oil
2 TB orange juice
2 TB white wine
2 TB white wine Worcestershire Sauce

- ❑ Preheat large cast iron skillet over medium high heat.
- ❑ In a large mixing bowl, toss peeled shrimp with 2 TB Seafood Serenade.
- ❑ Add oil to hot skillet and heat oil until just beginning to smoke.
- ❑ Sprinkle pan with remaining 1 tsp Seafood Serenade.
- ❑ Add shrimp to skillet, cook for 1-2 minutes on each side until shrimp are pink. Remove shrimp from pan.
- ❑ Add orange juice, wine, and Worcestershire whisking 1-2 minutes until reduced by half.
- ❑ Serve shrimp with pan drippings and cocktail sauce.

FOOL PROOF TIP: Sprinkling seasonings on a hot skillet prior to searing ensures better flavor transfer to product.

Slick E-Z Cocktail Sauce

6 oz ketchup
1 TB horseradish (prepared)
1 tsp Worcestershire Sauce
1/2 tsp Seafood Serenade
1/2 tsp lemon juice

- ❑ Mix thoroughly in a bowl. Chill in refrigerator.

FOOL PROOF TIP: All my spices can be used dry as a seasoning or rub. For a quick no-brainer marinade mix 1 tsp of your favorite Fool Proof flavor with 1 cup of Italian dressing.

Classic Steak House Onion Rings With BBQ Ranch Dip

1 large onion (cut into ½" rings)
1 C ice cubes
1 C buttermilk
3 TB Steak & Burger Rubdown
1 C all purpose flour
1 Qt corn oil or shortening

- In a large deep pot heat oil to 350°
- Place onion rings, ice cubes, buttermilk and 1 TB Steak & Burger in large bowl.
- In another large bowl, mix flour and remaining 2 TB Steak & Burger blending well.
- Remove onion from buttermilk and dredge in flour coating thoroughly.
- Deep fry in 350° oil until golden brown.
- Drain on paper and serve immediately with BBQ Ranch Dip or Mateo's Jalapeño Cream Mojo (p. 4)

BBQ Ranch Dip

8 oz sour cream
1 package ranch dressing mix
1/4 C BBQ sauce
1/4 tsp All Purpose Taste Massage
1 TB green onion (chopped fine)

- Mix thoroughly in a bowl.

FOOL PROOF TIP: Don't get stuck on the names, Fool Proof works on anything...Steak & Burger on grilled fish...Seafood Serenade for lemon chicken...All Purpose on french fries...Santa Fe on desserts...no, okay just kidding there. The point is use your imagination...it's Fool Proof!

Mi Casa Refried Bean Dip

1 can (16 oz) refried beans
1 C picante sauce
1 TB Santa Fe Sunset Blend

- ❑ Blend ingredients in a microwavable dish.
- ❑ Microwave on high for 2 minutes, stir, and microwave another minute.
- ❑ Serve dip hot or cold.

THE FOOL SUGGESTS: Besides a chip dip, this is a great topping ingredient in fajitas, tacos & nachos. Can also be a side dish when topped with bacon bits and cheddar cheese and baked until cheese is melted.

Pancho Villa's Queso Bueno

1/2 lb ground sirloin
1 TB + 1 tsp Santa Fe Sunset Blend
1½ lb Velveta cheese (diced)
1 can (10 oz) Rotel tomatoes (drained)
1 tsp green onion (minced)
2 tsp cilantro (chopped) optional

- ❑ In a sauté pan brown beef with 1 tsp Santa Fe and drain.
- ❑ Mix beef with cheese, tomatoes and 1 TB Santa Fe in microwavable bowl.
- ❑ Microwave 6 minutes stirring 3 times until cheese is melted and smooth.
- ❑ Stir in green onion and cilantro before serving.

FOOL PROOF TIP: Mix 1 TB of your favorite Fool Proof flavor per cup of cottage cheese for a *flavor fool* low fat dip or topping. Besides making boring raw veggies a taste treat, *Beverly Macki* of Arlington, Tx. says it's a great topper for a baked potato.

Roasted Mushroom
and Sweet Onion Tartlets

12 eggs
16 oz Half & Half
1/4 tsp nutmeg
1 TB Dijon mustard
24 large mushrooms (sliced)
1 sweet onion (sliced) best are Vidalia, Maui or Walla Walla
3 TB virgin olive oil
1 TB Steak & Burger Rubdown
1 lb Gruyere Swiss cheese (grated)
1/2 C Parmesan cheese (grated)
12 tartlet pastry shells

- ❑ Blend eggs, Half & Half, nutmeg and Dijon mustard in a bowl. Refrigerate for 1 hour.
- ❑ Preheat oven to 450°, preheat roasting pan for 10 minutes.
- ❑ Place mushrooms, onions, olive oil and Steak & Burger in preheated pan. Mix together well to coat mushrooms and onions.
- ❑ Place in preheated 450° oven for 5 minutes. Reduce oven temperature to 350° and cook for additional 20-30 minutes stirring occasionally to prevent sticking and burning.
- ❑ In a shallow baking dish place cooked mushroom mixture equally into tartlet shells and top with grated cheeses.
- ❑ Pour egg custard to fill. With a toothpick, stir slightly to incorporate egg mixture and release air pockets. Add more custard if stirring made room.
- ❑ Bake at 350° for 20-30 minutes until toothpick inserted in middle comes out clean.

THE FOOL SUGGESTS: Serve tarts on a bed of Tomato Marsala Gravy (p.30)

Brazilian Black Bean Soup

2 strips of bacon (diced small)
1 lb smoked ham (diced)
1 onion (diced small)
1 green bell pepper (diced small)
2 TB Santa Fe Sunset Blend
1 Qt chicken stock or broth
1/4 C maple syrup
1/4 C ketchup
2 (15 oz) cans black beans
1 bay leaf
1 tsp balsamic vinegar

- ❑ Defat bacon in large soup pot over medium heat. When bacon is crispy and brown remove from pot and reserve.
- ❑ Into bacon drippings add ham, onions, bell pepper and Santa Fe. Sauté until onion is tender.
- ❑ Add chicken stock, maple syrup, ketchup, black beans, bay leaf and crispy bacon. Bring to a boil for 10 minutes, stirring constantly to prevent sticking and scorching.
- ❑ Add vinegar, reduce heat to simmer, stirring occasionally for 30 min-1 hour until soup creams up and flavors strengthen.
- ❑ Serve topped with Mateo's Jalapeño Mojo (p.4) and Slick E-Z De Gallo.

Slick E-Z De Gallo

2 tomatoes (diced small)
1/2 onion (minced small)
4 TB cilantro (chopped)
1/2 fresh jalapeño (seeded & minced fine)
1 tsp Santa Fe Sunset Blend
1 lime (juiced)

- ❑ Mix all ingredients in bowl. Refrigerate to chill. Great low fat topping for chicken, nachos, baked potato, pasta or salad.

Sweet Loretta's Clam Chowder

12 strips bacon (chopped)
2 large onions (diced)
1 TB garlic (minced)
6 potatoes (diced) Ritter Critters prefer reds with skin on
4 large stalks of celery (diced)
4 large carrots (minced)
4 TB unsalted butter
4 TB flour
Approx 1 pt clam stock from steamed clams *or* juice from cans (add water to make up any difference)
3 C white wine
3 C water
1/2 bushel of clams (steamed & minced) *or* **3 large cans minced clams in juice**
4 C heavy cream
2 TB Seafood Serenade
1 TB black pepper
1 TB parsley (chopped fresh)

> "Be liberal! Be foolish. Enjoy! This recipe can be cut in half, but you'll hate yourself if you do!"
> Sweet Loretta

- In a large soup pot on medium heat defat bacon until crispy. Remove and reserve bacon.
- Return pot to stove. Sauté onion until transparent.
- Add garlic, potatoes, celery, carrots. Sauté until tender.
- Stir in butter. When melted add flour stirring until roux is thick and bubbly.
- Slowly add clam stock, wine and water stirring to prevent lumping. Bring to a boil.
- Add clams, crispy bacon, heavy cream, Seafood Serenade, pepper and parsley.
- Simmer for 1-3 hours stirring as needed to prevent sticking to bottom. *Do not scrape bottom of pot. Do not boil chowder after adding cream*

Loretta Ritter
Ritter Critter Barn & Fun House
Sunrise Lake, Pa.

Christine's Big Easy Oyster Artichoke Soup
It's Slick E-Z Too!

1/2 C unsalted butter
1 onion (chopped)
3 cloves garlic (chopped)
3 TB parsley (chopped)
2 tsp Seafood Serenade
2 cans (1 lb) artichoke hearts, drained & quartered
1 C oyster liquid (make up difference with sherry)
1 can (10¾ oz) cream of mushroom soup
1 bay leaf
1 Qt oysters (reserve liquid)
1 bunch green onion (chopped)

❑ In a large pot melt butter over low heat. Add onions and cook 4-5 minutes until soft.
❑ Add garlic, parsley and 1 tsp Seafood Serenade. Continue cooking for 2 minutes.
❑ Add artichoke hearts and cook 3 minutes more.
❑ Add oyster liquid, mushroom soup and bay leaf. Simmer 40 minutes over low heat, stirring as needed.
❑ Add oysters, green onions and season to taste with Seafood Serenade (*The Foolish Gourmet* likes 1 tsp) Simmer another 20 minutes.

THE FOOL SUGGESTS: Serve in soup plates with crusty French bread. For that genuine French Quarter touch, drizzle each soup bowl with ½ tsp warm, dry sherry.

Christine Dreyfus
Dreyfus Oyster House
Somewhere on the Water, U.S.A.

FOOL PROOF TIP: Popcorn takes on a new twist when you shake on Fool Proof instead of plain old salt.

South of the Border Cole Slaw

1/2 head green cabbage (shredded)
1/8 head red cabbage (shredded)
1/4 onion (minced)
2 stalks celery (minced)
2 carrots (shredded)
2 green onions (minced)
1/2 jalapeño (peeled, seeded, minced) optional
1 lemon (juiced)
3 TB powdered sugar
1/3 C olive oil
1/3 C red wine vinegar
1 TB Santa Fe Sunset Blend

❑ Mix all ingredients thoroughly in large mixing bowl.
❑ Refrigerate for two hours to steep flavors.
❑ Drain excess juices before serving.

Eileen's Favorite Potato Salad for Fools

6 potatoes (peeled, chopped and boiled)
3 eggs (hard boiled, peeled and chopped)
2 stalks celery (diced small)
1 (4 oz) jar pimentos (including juice)
2 green onions (chopped fine)
1½ C mayonnaise
1 TB mustard (heaping)
1/4 tsp granulated garlic
1 TB All Purpose Taste Massage
black pepper to taste

❑ Mix together in your favorite bowl. Refrigerate to chill.

Eileen Murphy, Ms. Yummo herself!
Charlotte, N.C.

Tortilla Crusted Chicken Salad
With Tomato Corn Relish & Santa Rosa Dressing

4 chicken breasts (boneless, skinless)
4 tsp Santa Fe Sunset Blend
1 C flour seasoned with 1 TB Santa Fe Sunset Blend
2 eggs (beaten)
1 C tortilla crumb breading (16 corn tortillas and 2 tsp
Santa Fe Sunset reduced to crumbs in food processor)
3 TB canola oil
4 C mixed salad greens (the fancier the better)

- ❑ Preheat oven to 350°
- ❑ Rub chicken breasts with 1 tsp Santa Fe per breast.
- ❑ Bread chicken by dredging in seasoned flour, patting off excess, dipping in beaten eggs, then dredge in seasoned tortilla crumbs.
- ❑ Sauté breaded chicken breasts in cast iron skillet with canola oil over medium heat until crumb finish is lightly golden brown on both sides.
- ❑ Transfer skillet to preheated oven and bake for 15-20 minutes to finish chicken. (internal temperature is 160°)
- ❑ Let chicken rest 5 minutes then slice and place on bed of salad greens. Top with Tomato Corn Relish & Santa Rosa Dressing

Tomato Corn Relish

2 tomatoes (diced small)
1 green bell pepper (diced small)
4 green onions (diced small)
1 C kernel corn
1 TB olive oil
2 limes (juiced)
1 TB sugar
1 TB Santa Fe Sunset Blend

- ❑ Toss ingredients in bowl and chill in refrigerator.

Santa Rosa Dressing

1/2 C mayonnaise
1/4 C ketchup
1 tsp Santa Fe Sunset Blend
2 TB water
1 green onion (chopped)
1 lime (juiced)
1 tsp cilantro (chopped) optional

❑ Mix all ingredients together. Chill in refrigerator.

Mother Would Rather Live at the Waldorf Chicken Salad

1 (8 oz) chicken breast (boneless skinless)
3 tsp Seafood Serenade
2 tsp olive oil
1 Granny Smith apple (diced)
1 red Delicious apple (diced)
1/2 C celery (diced)
1/2 C walnut halves & pieces
3/4 C mayonnaise
1 lemon (juiced)
2 TB powdered sugar

❑ Season chicken breasts with 2 tsp Seafood Serenade.
❑ Sauté chicken in olive oil and cook until done through (about 8 minutes) Dice then cool in refrigerator.
❑ In a large bowl mix remaining ingredients. Add diced chilled chicken.

THE FOOL SUGGESTS: Makes a great buffet salad item, a light salad for a stuffed pita or a refreshing summer salad on hearts of Romaine.

Lemon Scented Shrimp, Crab & Spinach Salad

24 shrimp (31-35 count, peeled, deveined)
8 oz lump crabmeat
5 tsp Seafood Serenade
2 TB olive oil
1 lemon (juiced)
1/2 red onion (thinly sliced)
8 oz fresh spinach (cleaned)
4 mushrooms (sliced)
1/2 red bell pepper (julienne)
2 tomatoes (cut into wedges)
1/2 cucumber (peeled, sliced thin)
1 TB parsley (fresh, chopped)

❏ Season shrimp with 4 tsp Seafood Serenade.
❏ Preheat skillet on stove top over high heat. Add olive oil and heat until just beginning to smoke. Sprinkle remaining tsp Seafood Serenade on skillet. Sauté shrimp until cooked pink through and just loosely curled. Deglaze with lemon juice. Remove from pan immediately to large bowl.
❏ Add crab meat and chopped parsley to bowl. Toss lightly so as not to break up crab but mixing well all ingredients.
❏ Arrange spinach on 4 plates with cut vegetables. Arrange seafood on top. Serve with Honey Mustard Dressing (p.19)

Slick E-Z French Dressing

1/2 C olive oil
1/4 C red vinegar
1/4 C ketchup
2 TB water
2 tsp All Purpose Taste Massage
1/2 tsp granulated garlic
1 tsp soy sauce

❏ Mix in a jar. Shake well before serving.

Grilled Ancho Chicken Salad

4 (4-5 oz) chicken breasts (boneless, skinless)
1 C honey
2 C chile sauce can substitute ketchup
1 C mixed nuts (roasted, salted)
1/2 C + 2 tsp olive oil
1/4 C tequila
3 dried ancho peppers (seeded, soaked in warm water 1 hr)
1/4 C red wine vinegar
2 TB garlic (chopped)
2 TB Santa Fe Sunset Blend
8 oz fancy mixed salad greens
2 C crispy tortilla strips (baked or fried)
12 tomato wedges
1 TB cilantro (chopped)

❑ In a blender or food processor purée softened peppers, honey, nuts, tequila, chile sauce, vinegar, garlic and 1 TB Santa Fe Sunset Blend.

❑ Add olive oil to mixture slowly while machine is on to blend dressing. Dressing is to be of a thick consistency but if it's too thick, thin with 1-2 tablespoons of water. Cover and chill in refrigerator.

❑ Toss chicken breasts in 2 tsp olive oil and 1 TB Santa Fe. Let rest for 20 minutes while preparing hot grill.

❑ Grill chicken over high heat for 3 minutes on each side. Move chicken to medium heat, continuing cooking for 12-15 minutes turning twice more.

❑ Let chicken rest 3-5 minutes, then slice and place in large salad bowl. Add greens and enough dressing to coat. Toss together then place on salad plates. Garnish with tortilla strips, tomato wedges and chopped cilantro.

Greg Provine, Executive Chef
Holiday Inn Select North
Dallas, Tx.

Pacific Rim Vinegarette

1/2 C canola oil
1 TB sesame oil
1/4 C rice vinegar
2 TB ketchup
3 TB soy sauce
1 TB toasted sesame seeds
1 tsp granulated garlic
1/4 tsp ginger powder
2 TB water
2 TB lt. brown sugar
1 tsp Steak & Burger Rubdown
1/4 tsp black pepper (fresh ground recommended)

❑ Mix thoroughly in a shaker jar.

FOOLISH NOTE: If your house is like most and you have a ba-zillion bottles of salad dressing just to have a variety, you'll really enjoy my Slick E-Z dressings. You can whip them up quickly in small quantities and free up a lot of refrigerator space. See also Santa Rosa (p.16) and Slick E-Z French on (p.17)

Honey Mustard Dressing

4 oz bacon (minced)
1¼ C mayonnaise or Miracle Whip
1/4 C prepared mustard
3/4 C honey
1 TB red onion (minced fine)
1 TB green onion tops (minced)
1 TB parsley (chopped)
1 tsp Steak & Burger Rubdown
2 tsp white wine vinegar

❑ Cook minced bacon in large bowl in microwave for 8 minutes stirring 4 times until crispy.
❑ Cool bacon and grease to room temperature.
❑ Add remaining ingredients and mix well. Chill.

Producers' Club Open Faced Steak Sandwich

12 slices tenderloin of beef (cut in 2 oz medallions)
2 TB Steak & Burger Rubdown
1 TB olive oil
2 C Ruby Port wine
2 TB shallot (minced)
6 mushrooms (sliced, sautéed with 1 tsp olive oil, 1 tsp Steak & Burger Rubdown and ¼ tsp nutmeg)
1 can cream of mushroom soup
1 TB beef bouillon granules
1 TB unsalted butter
3 slices pumpernickel bread

- Preheat skillet on stove top over medium high heat.
- Season tenderloin with 2 TB Steak & Burger Rubdown.
- Add half of olive oil to skillet, heat until just smoking. Sear half of beef medallions on both sides, remove from pan, reserve on platter to capture beef juices. Repeat process to sear remaining medallions.
- Return skillet to stove. Deglaze pan with port wine, reduce by half scraping brown bits from pan bottom.
- Add cream of mushroom, sautéed mushrooms and bouillon, bring to a boil, reduce to simmer for 5 minutes.
- Toast bread and cut into quarters on the diagonal.
- Return steak medallions and their rendered juices to skillet to heat beef.
- Assemble plates layering 3 slices each of toast and beef in alternating fashion (you can even build a tower)
- Return pan to stove, whisk in butter until melted and sauce is smooth. Spoon over sandwiches to serve. *Great formal luncheon served with red potatoes and asparagus.*

FOOL PROOF TIP: Add All Purpose Taste Massage to your favorite tuna salad recipe. You decide how much you like. I promise it'll make your tuna tunier!

Truck Stop Jack's
Philly Cheese Steak Sandwich

4 TB olive oil
2 lb top round of beef (sliced very thin, raw)
2 TB Steak & Burger Rubdown
1/2 onion (sliced thin julienne)
6 mushrooms (sliced, sautéed)
1 green bell pepper (sliced thin)
1 lb Provolone cheese (sliced)
6 hoagie rolls

❑ In a large skillet place olive oil and heat until just beginning to smoke.
❑ Add sliced beef and Steak & Burger, cook, stirring until browned.
❑ Add onion, mushrooms and peppers. Cook until tender.
❑ Toast hoagie rolls with 2½ oz. Provolone cheese in each roll.
❑ Load beef mixture into rolls.

FOOLISH NOTE: Serve wrapped in butcher paper for the authentic flavor of the street, however don't eat the paper or lick the street.

This recipe is included in memory of our dear friend Jack DeGennaro who was a trucker from Philadelphia and knew a good cheese steak when he bit one! It's a feel good sandwich just like Jack was a feel good kinda guy.

A FOOLISH WORD: You may have noticed by now Fool Proof Tips may not have anything to do with the page they're on. You're right! They're just some things I'd like for you to know.

FOOL PROOF TIP: To add a different dimension of flavor to your sauces and gravies, whisk a teaspoon of jelly or Dijon mustard into the sauce at the end of procedure.

"I'm No Turkey," Turkey Burger
(but just watch 'em gobble these)

1¼ lb ground turkey
1/3 C onion (minced)
1/3 C green bell pepper (minced)
3 TB ketchup
2 egg yolks
1 tsp Worcestershire Sauce
1 TB Steak & Burger Rubdown
2 tsp mustard
1/2 C whole wheat bread crumbs (fresh)
1 tsp soy sauce
4 TB canola oil

- Combine all ingredients *except* canola oil in large bowl. Mix well. Portion mixture into four 6 oz. patties.
- Preheat large skillet on stove top on medium heat.
- Add canola oil to skillet and heat another 2 minutes.
- Sprinkle each patty with ¼ tsp Steak & Burger.
- Cook 15 minutes turning several times to prevent sticking.

Everything's Bigger in Texas Taters

6 baking potatoes
2 TB + 2 tsp All Purpose Taste Massage
1/4 C vegetable oil

- Preheat oven to 350°
- Cut potatoes lengthwise into wedges, quarters or sixths depending on potato size. Mix 2 TB All Purpose Taste Massage with oil and toss potatoes in seasoned oil.
- Place on baking sheet, skin side down. Sprinkle entire pan with remaining 2 tsp All Purpose to zest up Taters.
- Bake for 50-60 minutes until inside of potatoes is soft and outside is crisp and brown.

Angus Beef Tenderloin Saltimboca
With Fingerling Mashed Potatoes
And Crispy Leeks

2 lb Angus beef tenderloin (cut in 12 medallions)
24 slices Prosciutto ham
24 asparagus spears (blanched in boiling water 1 minute)
1 C basil (fresh, coarsely chopped)
3 cloves garlic (chopped)
3 TB olive oil
2 TB Steak & Burger Rubdown

- ❏ Sauté basil and garlic in 2 TB oil. Cool and reserve.
- ❏ Lay medallions on hard surface, season all with 1 TB Steak & Burger. Place a slice of ham on each. Pound with a meat mallet until meat is ¼" thick.
- ❏ Rub basil garlic mixture, divided evenly, on pounded slices.
- ❏ Roll slices (garlic and ham will be to the inside) around 2 pieces of asparagus and secure with a toothpick. Season all with 1 TB Steak & Burger.
- ❏ Heat 1 TB olive oil in a skillet on stove top over high heat until just beginning to smoke.
- ❏ Sauté beef rolls on all sides approx 2-3 minutes until medium rare. Set aside and keep warm for presentation.

Bernhard Muller, Executive Chef
Four Seasons Resort and Club
Las Colinas, Tx.

FOOL PROOF TIP: Blanching is to cook an item very briefly in boiling water or in hot fat. It's used to loosen peels, cook partially to make ready for another step, prepare for freezing or to remove undesirable flavors. Blanching is an easy way to prepare certain dense vegetables for grilling or stir frying. As you become familiar with this technique you will save cooking time and improve results in your recipes.

Fingerling Mashed Potatoes and Crispy Leeks

1 lb Fingerling potatoes
1/2 lb Idaho potatoes
1 C buttermilk
1 tsp olive oil
2 tsp Steak & Burger Rubdown
2 C leeks (white part, washed, cut julienne)
2 C carrots (julienne)
1/2 C Tempura flour (seasoned with 1 TB Steak & Burger)
18 baby beets (blanched, sautéed in butter)
2 C canola or peanut oil

❑ Cook 2 varieties of potatoes separately in salted water until tender.
❑ Mash together with buttermilk, olive oil and 2 tsp Steak & Burger. Place in ziplock plastic bag and keep warm.
❑ Preheat 2 C oil in fryer or deep skillet to 325°
❑ Toss carrots and leeks in seasoned Tempura flour to coat. Fry until crispy. Drain on paper.

Presentation: Cut corner in the bag of mashed potatoes making it a disposable pastry bag. Pipe potatoes onto 6 warm plates. Cut one beef roll in half and place on each side of potatoes. Place another roll on top of potatoes. Garnish sides of beef with 3 beets and drizzle Rosemary Port Glace (p.53) over plate.

Bernhard Muller, Executive Chef
Four Seasons Resort and Club
Las Colinas, Tx.

FOOL PROOF TIP: Whisking a teaspoon of unsalted butter into sauces and gravies prior to serving will impart a rich finish.

Roast Prime Rib of Beef Au Jus

1/2 rack ribeye roast (approx 8 lb)
8 TB Steak & Burger Rubdown

- ❑ Preheat oven to 400°
- ❑ Rub roast with 1 TB olive oil. Apply Steak & Burger generously and rub in well (if possible refrigerate overnight)
- ❑ Place remaining 2 TB olive oil in a very hot roasting pan on top of stove. Sear roast on all sides.
- ❑ Transfer roast in pan to 400° oven for 10 minutes. Reduce heat to 275° and cook until internal temperature in middle of roast is 125° for medium rare , or 130° for medium.
- ❑ Remove roast from oven as well as from pan and allow to rest on a large platter for 20 minutes.
- ❑ Reserve roasting pan for Au Jus Sauce.

Au Jus Sauce

1/2 onion (diced large)
1 stalk celery (diced large)
1 carrot (diced large)
4 cloves garlic (smashed)
1 C white wine
2 tsp corn starch
1 C water
2 TB beef bouillon granules
1 bay leaf

- ❑ Pour off fat from pan, leaving the brown bits and drippings *reserving poured off fat for Yorkshire Pudding*
- ❑ Place roasting pan on stove on medium high heat. Add onion, celery, carrot and garlic. Sauté until vegetables are brown and caramelized.
- ❑ Add white wine and reduce volume by half.
- ❑ Mix corn starch, water and beef bouillon in a bowl. Stir this mixture along with bay leaf into sauce.

- Reduce temperature and simmer for 5 minutes whisking in brown bits from sides and bottom of pan into sauce.
- Strain sauce before serving.

Yorkshire Pudding

1 C all purpose flour (sifted)
1 tsp salt
1 C whole milk
1 C cold water
4 eggs (lightly beaten)
2 TB roast beef fat drippings

- Preheat oven to 500°
- Mix flour and salt in bowl. Add milk slowly, stirring until smooth.
- Add water and eggs beating until frothy. Cover with a cloth loosely and let stand on a cool counter for a half hour. Later whip batter again until bubbly.
- Pour ½ tsp roast fat drippings into each of 12 muffin pan cups. Place muffin pan into hot oven until drippings are almost smoking (approx. 2 minutes)
- Portion 3 TB batter into each cup. Bake 8 minutes at 500° *Do not open oven door during this 8 minutes.* Reduce temperature to 400° and bake 8-10 minutes longer until well browned and risen.
- Arrange these delicious pudding breads around roast and serve immediately.

FOOLISH NOTE: This recipe can be divided or multiplied, just be sure you have plenty of sauce for sopping.

FOOL PROOF TIP: Ever notice the flavor and quality of meats sautéed in a fine restaurant? Here's how the big boys do it. Begin process by preheating skillet on stove top over medium-high to high heat depending on cut of meat. Sear meat on all sides. Finish cooking in a very hot (400°- 450°) oven.

Towering Tenderloin of Beef and Shrimp

2 lb beef tenderloin
2 TB + 1 tsp Steak & Burger Rubdown
12 large shrimp (25 ct, peeled and deveined)
1 TB All Purpose Taste Massage
1 TB olive oil
1 sweet potato (cooked, sliced into ½" rounds)
2 large tomatoes (sliced)

- Preheat skillet on stove top at medium high heat.
- Slice tenderloin into 8 medallions and rub with 2 TB Steak & Burger.
- Season shrimp with 2 tsp All Purpose Taste Massage.
- Add 1 tsp olive oil to hot pan, sauté beef medallions searing all around. Remove from pan when done to your liking. Reserve to a platter to capture juices.
- Add another 1 tsp olive oil to pan. Heat until just beginning to smoke. Sprinkle bottom of skillet with remaining 1 tsp All Purpose. *This adds flavor transfer in the sauté process.*
- Add shrimp to skillet sautéing until done (pink & firm) Remove and reserve.
- Return skillet to stove. Add remaining 1 tsp olive oil.
- Season sweet potato medallions and tomato slices with remaining 1 tsp Steak & Burger. Sauté in hot skillet until brown.
- Remove and assemble beef towers on individual plates alternating potato, beef, tomato, ending with beef. Garnish with shrimp around beef tower. Pour Slick E-Z Beef Glaze over tower and serve.

FOOL PROOF TIP: Use your favorite Fool Proof flavor to make seasoned flour or breadcrumbs. Simply mix 2 tablespoons of Fool Proof to 1 cup of flour, meal or crumbs.

Slick E-Z Beef Glaze

1/2 C mushrooms (sautéed in ½ tsp olive oil with 1 tsp Steak & Burger Rubdown)
1/4 C dry sherry
1 C water
2 TB beef bouillon granules
2 tsp corn starch
1 TB unsalted butter

- ❑ Mix ingredients *except butter* well in a bowl.
- ❑ Pour and whisk into hot skillet of pan drippings from sautéed beef and shrimp. Bring to a boil then reduce to a simmer for 3 minutes.
- ❑ Whisk 1 TB butter into glaze before removing from heat.
- ❑ Pour over tenderloin of beef.

Corona Del Mar Spoon Bread

1 C Bisquick flour
1 C corn meal
2 eggs
1/4 C beer (not light)
1/2 C buttermilk
1 TB Santa Fe Sunset Blend
2 tsp sugar
1/2 C kernel corn
1 TB cilantro optional

- ❑ Mix ingredients in a large bowl.
- ❑ Drop spoons full of batter into 350° cooking oil. Fry until golden brown and floating.
- ❑ Sprinkle with Santa Fe immediately after removing from oil to drain on paper towel.

FOOL PROOF TIP: Can be used as a batter for fried shrimp, vegetables, scallops and chicken fingers. Way yummo amigo!

Fool Proof Steak Loaf

2 lb ground sirloin
1/2 C onion (minced)
1/2 C green bell pepper (diced)
2 TB + 1 tsp Steak & Burger Rubdown
3 egg yolks
2 whole eggs
1/4 C ketchup
2 TB mustard (Dijon whole grain)
1 tsp prepared horseradish optional
2 tsp Worcestershire Sauce
1 C bread crumbs (fresh, white bread)
1 tsp soy sauce

❑ Preheat oven to 350°
❑ Combine ingredients *except the 1 tsp Steak & Burger.* Mix well.
❑ Form into loaf or place in loaf pan. Sprinkle remaining Steak & Burger on top of loaf.
❑ Bake in 350° oven for 35 minutes.
❑ Remove from oven, cover with 1/2 C Tomato Marsala Gravy.
❑ Return to oven for an additional 25 minutes (internal temperature is 160°)

Slick E-Z Version: You can eliminate Tomato Marsala topping and simply bake 60 minutes. It's still a *great* meat loaf, but with the Marsala it's the *best* meat loaf!

THE FOOL SUGGESTS: Serve with mashed potatoes and green peas. Leftovers make wonderful open faced sandwich topped with Tomato Marsala Gravy.

FOOL PROOF TIP: Amount of spice for seasoning is a personal taste. I recommend 1 tablespoon per pound of meats.

Tomato Marsala Gravy

1/2 C onion (diced)
2 tsp All Purpose Taste Massage
3 tsp garlic (chopped)
2 tsp olive oil
1/2 C Marsala wine
2 TB beef bouillon granules
2 TB lt. brown sugar
3 TB all purpose flour
3 C crushed tomatoes
2 TB fresh basil (chopped) optional
2 TB unsalted butter optional

❑ In microwavable bowl, mix onion, All Purpose Taste Massage, garlic and olive oil. Microwave 2 minutes.
❑ Add Marsala, beef bouillon, sugar and flour in that order. Mix well. Add tomatoes. Blend again. Return to microwave for 10 minutes stirring 3 times. Add fresh basil and butter.

Buttermilk Country Gravy

1/4 lb mild Italian Sausage
1/2 C onion (minced)
2 TB canola oil
1/2 C flour
1 TB chicken bouillon granules
1 C buttermilk
1 tsp Steak & Burger Rubdown
1/4 tsp All Purpose Taste Massage

❑ Mince sausage and microwave on high 3 minutes stirring three times.
❑ Drain. Chop again very fine.
❑ Add onions and oil. Microwave 2 minutes stirring twice.
❑ Whisk in flour. Microwave 2 minutes stirring twice.
❑ Add buttermilk, bouillon and seasonings. Microwave 6 minutes stirring 5 times.

Philadelphia Yankee Crock Roast

5-6 lb beef roast (eye of the round preferred)
2 TB Steak & Burger Rubdown
1 TB olive oil
1 large onion (diced)
12 mushrooms (quartered)
1 C Ruby Port wine
1 C all purpose flour
4 C water
4 TB beef bouillon granules
1/2 C ketchup
1/2 C tomatoes (diced, drained of excess moisture)

- ❑ Preheat crock pot on high setting.
- ❑ Rub Steak & Burger on roast.
- ❑ Add olive oil to pot, sear roast in oil on all sides.
- ❑ Add onions and mushrooms to sauté. Continue to cook until onions are soft.
- ❑ In a large bowl, mix all remaining ingredients stirring to make sure flour is totally dissolved. Add to crock pot. Add additional water to cover if needed.
- ❑ Bring pot to a boil for 1 hour.
- ❑ Reduce heat to low and cover with lid. Cook on low 4-6 hours until tender stirring occasionally if possible. *Roast is done when you can stick in and twist a fork and the meat easily pulls apart.*

THE FOOL SUGGESTS: Great with buttered egg noodles. Makes fantastic hot open faced sandwiches.

FOOL PROOF TIP: When grilling meats, sear on all sides on a hot part of the grill to lock in juices and flavors, then move to a lower temperature area of the grill or to an oven to finish the cooking process. The oven is nice 'cause you have more temperature control, no need to tend it. At the grill have a spray bottle of water handy to cool it down as needed.

Can't Beat It, BBQ Brisket
Slick E-Z Method

10 lb beef brisket
10 TB All Purpose Taste Massage

❑ Rub brisket with 10 TB of All Purpose Taste Massage. Wrap in plastic and store overnight in refrigerator. *Do not trim the fat off the brisket. This will ensure a very moist and tender brisket*

Brisket Baster

1 C balsamic vinegar
1/4 C Worcestershire Sauce
1/2 C soy sauce
1/2 C lt. brown sugar
1 TB All Purpose Taste Massage
1 TB black pepper (fresh ground)
1 C red wine
1 TB liquid smoke

❑ Preheat oven to 450° while mixing all of the Baster ingredients together in a bowl.
❑ Sear seasoned brisket on all sides over hot grill.
❑ Place on roasting pan and transfer to 450° oven for 15 minutes. Reduce heat to 275° for 9 hours until internal temperature is 190-200° basting with Brisket Baster every 30 minutes as much as possible.

FOOLISH NOTE: If using a smoker, sear brisket over grill then transfer to smoker, basting continuously as above. Smokers allow a lot of creativity in flavoring. Consider throwing in that apple tree branch from pruning, or rosemary cuttings. Pecan shells or mesquite tree seed pods give yet another flavor possibility. Let your imagination work for you but if you're considering adding Uncle Fred's tennis shoe, stop!

Orange Beef and Pepper Stir Fry

2 lb beef tips (sirloin is best)
1 TB Steak & Burger Rubdown
2 TB peanut oil
1/2 tsp sesame oil
1 tsp ginger (fresh, grated)
1 TB garlic (minced)
1 onion (diced)
1 red bell pepper (diced)
1 green bell pepper (diced)
2 oranges (sectioned)
1/2 tsp Seafood Serenade
Wok About Sauce Pot (recipe below)

- Preheat skillet over high heat. Rub beef with Steak & Burger.
- Add 1 TB peanut oil and ¼ tsp sesame oil to skillet. Heat until just beginning to smoke. Sear beef tips off. Remove and reserve on plate to collect juices.
- Return skillet to stove until hot. Add remaining oil, ginger, garlic, onion and bell peppers. Sauté retaining crispness.
- Add oranges, Seafood Serenade and Wok About Sauce Pot.
- Bring to a boil and immediately reduce heat. Return beef and any juices rendered to pan.
- Simmer for 2 minutes. Serve over rice.

Wok About Sauce Pot

1/2 C orange juice
1/2 C water
1/2 C red wine
3 TB soy sauce
2 TB corn starch
2 TB ketchup
2 TB sugar

- Mix together in bowl, microwave on high for 3 minutes stirring twice.

Santa Fe Beef and Peppers

1½ lb flank steak
2 TB Santa Fe Sunset Blend
2 TB olive oil
2 TB strong coffee
1½ C sherry
2 TB picante sauce
1 pkg Knorr Demi Glace Mix
2 TB ketchup
1 C water
1/2 onion (julienne)
1/2 red bell pepper (cut in strips)
1/2 yellow bell pepper (cut in strips)
1/2 green bell pepper (cut in strips)
2 TB cilantro (chopped)
1 tomato (cut in wedges)

❑ Preheat skillet on high heat and oven to 450°
❑ Rub flank steak with 1 TB Santa Fe and 1 TB olive oil.
❑ Add 1 tsp olive oil to skillet until almost smoking. Sprinkle pan with 1 tsp Santa Fe, then sear flank on both sides. Place skillet of beef in preheated oven for 8 minutes.
❑ Remove from oven. Let stand for 15 minutes, then slice beef in strips across the grain.
❑ In a microwavable bowl mix coffee, sherry, picante, demi glace mix, ketchup and water. Microwave mixture for 5 minutes stirring twice. Set aside.
❑ Return skillet to stove top to heat on medium high. Add remaining 2 tsp olive oil to hot skillet. Add onion, peppers, and 2 tsp Santa Fe sautéing for approx. 2 minutes.
❑ Add bowl of microwaved sauce to skillet. Bring to a boil.
❑ Add tomatoes, beef and cilantro. Reduce heat to simmer 3 additional minutes. Serve over Spanish Rice (p.36)

FOOL PROOF TIP: Add Santa Fe Sunset Blend to your favorite chile recipe, eggs, and fajita meats. Wonderful for table top when some of the family likes it hot and some do not!

Beef Burritos Grande

1/2 lb ground sirloin
1/2 C onion (diced)
1 TB Santa Fe Sunset Blend
1 tomato (diced)
1/2 C red bell pepper (diced)
1 avocado (cut in strips)
1 C Monterey Jack cheese (grated)
1 TB cilantro (chopped)
6 large flour tortillas

❑ Spray with oil and preheat skillet on medium-low heat.
❑ Brown beef with onion and Santa Fe. Add tomato and bell pepper. Sauté until tender.
❑ Assemble burritos by placing beef filling, avocado, cheese and cilantro dividing filling equally among 6 tortillas and roll first folding in ends to contain filling.
❑ Spray pan. Grill burritos on both sides until golden brown and cheese is melted. Serve with Corn & Tomato Salsa.

Summer Corn and Tomato Salsa

1 C kernel corn
1 C tomato (diced)
1/4 C green onion (chopped)
2 TB vinegar
2 TB corn starch
2 TB sugar
2 TB white wine
2 TB water
2 TB Santa Fe Sunset Blend
1 tsp cilantro (chopped)

❑ In a large microwavable bowl mix ingredients thoroughly.
❑ Microwave on high 4 minutes, stirring 3 times.

Spanish Rice

1 strip bacon (minced) optional
1 TB olive oil
3 tsp Santa Fe Sunset Blend
1/2 C onion (diced)
1/4 C green bell pepper (diced)
1/4 C red bell pepper (diced)
1 C kernel corn
1 tomato (diced)
1/2 C black beans (canned, drained and rinsed)
3 C cooked rice
2 green onions (chopped)
1 TB cilantro (chopped)

❑ Preheat large skillet on stove top over medium high heat.
❑ Add minced bacon and olive oil. Sauté until bacon is browned but not crispy.
❑ Add 1 tsp Santa Fe, onion, bell peppers. Sauté until tender, stirring often.
❑ Add another 1 tsp Santa Fe and corn. Sauté 1 minute to release flavors.
❑ Add 3rd tsp Santa Fe, tomato, and black beans. Cook until mixture is almost dry of liquid.
❑ Add cooked rice, stirring until rice is hot.
❑ Add green onion and cilantro to pan just before serving.

Slick E-Z Rice

1½ C water per 1 C rice

❑ Place water and rice in a deep microwavable bowl. Add *optional* butter and salt. Cover with tight fitting lid. Microwave on high 8 minutes. Let rest a *minimum* of 2 minutes (can be as long as needed). Stir. Microwave another 8 minutes.
❑ For seasoned rice, stir 1 TB of your favorite Fool Proof seasoning into water. *Spanish Rice is already seasoned.*

London Broil Florentine

1 flank steak (12-16 oz)
1 TB All Purpose Taste Massage
2 TB olive oil
6 mushrooms (sliced)
4 oz fresh spinach
1 tsp Steak & Burger Rubdown
2 oz Boursin cheese

- ❑ Preheat oven to 450° and skillet on stove top. Rub flank steak with All Purpose Taste Massage.
- ❑ Add 1 TB olive oil to hot skillet. Sear flank on both sides. Remove from pan and set aside on platter to reserve juices.
- ❑ In the same pan sauté mushrooms in remaining TB of olive oil for 2 minutes.
- ❑ Add spinach and Steak & Burger. Sauté another minute.
- ❑ Remove spinach mixture to cool in refrigerator.
- ❑ Cut flank steak lengthwise to form pocket. Stuff with spinach mixture and Boursin cheese.
- ❑ Roast stuffed steak for 10-15 minutes in a 450° oven. Remove and let rest for 10 minutes before slicing.
- ❑ Serve with Brown Sherry Crème.

Brown Sherry Crème

1 C water
1 TB sherry
1/4 C onion (minced)
4 mushrooms (chopped)
1 TB beef bouillon
1 TB corn starch
1/2 tsp Steak & Burger Rubdown
1 TB sour cream
1 TB unsalted butter

- ❑ Combine ingredients *except sour cream and butter* in microwavable bowl. Mix well.
- ❑ Microwave on high for 6 minutes, stirring twice.
- ❑ Add sour cream and butter whisking until smooth.

Fool Proof Turkey Dinner

3½ lb turkey breast (half the breast)
2 TB All Purpose Taste Massage
1 TB olive oil

❑ Preheat oven to 350° and a skillet on stove top over medium high heat.
❑ Rub turkey with oil and All Purpose Taste Massage. Sear on all sides. Place in preheated oven.
❑ Roast for 45-55 minutes until internal temperature is 160°

NO FOOLIN': For a great, *juicy* turkey, de-bone whole turkey (your butcher can do this for you if you ask real nice) Rub well with All Purpose Taste Massage at a rate of 1 TB per pound of turkey. Roast in preheated 350° oven. It will take only 1 hour to roast and will be *the juiciest* turkey ever because the bones aren't there to draw juice from the meat. Let rest for 20 minutes before slicing to insure maximum flavor and juiciness.

Slick E-Z Turkey Gravy

1 C water
1 C onion (diced)
1/2 C white wine or dry vermouth
1/2 tsp All Purpose Taste Massage
2 cans cream of chicken soup

❑ Pour off fat from roasting pan reserving brown bits. Return pan to stove top on medium heat. Sauté onion in drippings until browned (approx 2 minutes) being careful not to burn.
❑ Whisk white wine into pan and reduce by half.
❑ Add cream of chicken soup, water and All Purpose to pan. Simmer 20 minutes.

THE FOOL SUGGESTS: Serve with Rosie's All Occassion Rice Stuffing, Parmesan Pull-Apart Bread and Cranberry Corn Relish on following pages.

Rosie's All Occasion Anytime Rice Stuffing

1/4 lb bacon (minced)
1/2 onion (diced medium)
3 stalks celery (diced medium)
1/2 C red bell pepper (diced medium)
1/2 C green bell pepper (diced medium)
1 TB garlic (chopped)
3 mushrooms (sliced)
1/2 C raisins
1/4 lb sausage (cooked, diced medium) Italian is best
2 TB All Purpose Taste Massage
2 apples (skin on, diced medium) 1 red & 1 Granny Smith
1 orange (sectioned)
1/4 tsp orange zest
3 C rice (cooked)
1 egg (lightly beaten)

❑ Defat bacon in large skillet on medium heat. Remove when brown and crispy.

❑ To same skillet add onion, celery, bell pepper, garlic, mushroom, raisins and sausage. Sauté until vegetable are tender and raisins are plump.

❑ Add All Purpose, apples, oranges, orange zest and cooked rice. Sauté for additional 5 minutes until ingredients are blended and hot.

❑ Add egg to mixture. Cook additional 3-5 minutes stirring constantly until egg is cooked and mixture takes on a stuffing consistency.

❑ Option 1: Bake stuffing in casserole dish for 20 minutes at 300° for great tasting side dish.

❑ Option 2: If you must…stuff your turkey, but *The Foolish Gourmet* objects to stuffing turkeys because it produces a dry product at best, *and* the turkey doesn't like it much either!

A lot of this stuffing was made in Roseann's pan on the cover.

Parmesan Pull-Apart Bread

1 pkg frozen Parker House rolls (thawed)
1/4 C unsalted butter (melted)
2 C Parmesan cheese (fresh, grated)
1 TB All Purpose Taste Massage
1/4 tsp garlic powder

- Preheat oven to 375° Grease a fluted bundt pan.
- Mix together cheese, All Purpose and garlic powder.
- Dip each roll in butter, then roll in cheese mixture to coat.
- Place coated dough evenly around pan. Allow dough to rise until double in size.
- Bake in 375° oven for 30-40 until well browned and top of bread is crisp and sounds hollow when tapped.
- Remove immediately from pan to cool on wire rack.

Cranberry Corn Relish

1 TB olive oil
2 tsp All Purpose Taste Massage
1/2 onion (diced small)
2 stalks celery (diced small)
1/2 C red bell pepper (diced medium)
1/2 C green bell pepper (diced medium)
3 C corn
1 pkg (12 oz) cranberries (fresh)
2 C sugar
1 C orange juice
1 C dry vermouth
1 TB corn starch

- Preheat large pot on stove top over medium heat.
- Sauté onion, celery, and bell pepper, in olive oil and All Purpose for 1 minute.
- Add corn, cranberries, sugar and orange juice.
- In a bowl, dissolve corn starch in vermouth and stir into pot. Bring to a boil. Reduce to a simmer for 10 minutes.

Rodeo Drive BBQ Chicken Pizza

2 boneless skinless chicken breasts (approx 8-10 oz)
4 tsp Santa Fe Sunset Blend
2 tsp olive oil
1 can pizza dough (rolled thin)
1/2 C Rodeo Q Sauce
1 C sharp cheddar cheese (grated)
1 C mozzarella cheese (grated)
1 C Parmesan cheese (grated)
1/2 green bell pepper (julienned)
1/2 onion (julienned)

- ❏ Preheat oven to 425°
- ❏ Cook chicken breasts with 2 tsp Santa Fe and 1 tsp olive oil.
- ❏ Roll pizza dough thin. Spread 1 tsp olive oil on dough. Bake at 425° for 7 minutes.
- ❏ Spread Rodeo Q Sauce on dough to your liking (The Fool likes 1/2 cup)
- ❏ In a bowl combine cheeses with 2 tsp Santa Fe. Sprinkle mixture on pizza.
- ❏ Slice chicken. Spread on top with onions and peppers. Bake 10 minutes.

Rodeo Q Sauce

1 C ketchup
1/4 C lt. brown sugar
1 TB Santa Fe Sunset Blend
1/4 tsp liquid smoke
1 tsp Worcestershire Sauce
1 lime (juiced)
1 tsp balsamic vinegar

- ❏ Mix well in bowl. Microwave 3 minutes stirring once.

THE FOOL SUGGESTS: Rodeo Q is excellent on chicken or pork chops seasoned with good old Santa Fe.

Twelve Minutes to Health Chicken
Slick E-Z Chicken Breast

6 boneless skinless chicken breasts
3½ tsp of your favorite Fool Proof seasoning
2 tsp canola oil

- ❑ Season chicken with ½ tsp Fool Proof per breast.
- ❑ Heat skillet on stove top on high *and* preheat oven to 450°
- ❑ Add canola oil to pan and heat until just beginning to smoke.
- ❑ Sprinkle remaining ½ tsp Fool Proof on surface of pan. Add chicken to pan searing on both sides (approx 2 minutes per side). Move skillet to preheated oven and finish cooking (approx 8 minutes). *Cooking time depends on thickness of breasts.* Squeezing a lemon, lime, orange or tablespoon of wine over chicken just before removing from pan will add a burst of flavor.
- ❑ Let rest a few minutes before serving to insure juiciness.

FOOL PROOF TIP: This cooking technique works for pork chops as well although cook them 10 minutes in the oven.

FOOLISH NOTE: I have designed Fool Proof's seasoning blends to give you complex flavor simply. Just shake them on any product and roast, bake or sauté. Go ahead, Make It Fool Proof!

Zesty Butter for Any Occasion

2 TB unsalted butter
1/2 tsp Seafood Serenade
1/4 tsp vermouth
1/4 tsp orange zest (finely grated)
1/2 tsp chives (fresh, chopped fine)

- ❑ Combine all ingredients well in a bowl. Chill.

Mandarin Chicken Stir Fry

2 lb chicken thigh meat (boned and skinned)
1 TB All Purpose Taste Massage
1 TB peanut oil
1/8 tsp sesame oil
1/2 C onion (diced large)
1 TB garlic (chopped)
1/2 tsp fresh ginger (grated fine)
1/8 tsp red pepper flakes optional
1/2 C green onion (sliced ½" long)
1 orange (skinned, sliced in cross sections)
No Genius Khan Sauce Pot

❑ Cut thigh meat into 1" pieces, place in bowl. Season with All Purpose.
❑ Preheat large skillet on high heat, add peanut and sesame oil. Heat until just beginning to smoke.
❑ Add chicken, sauté, stirring quickly for approx. 2 minutes until browned.
❑ Add onion, garlic, ginger and red pepper flakes. Continue to sauté stirring quickly for 1-2 minutes.
❑ Add Genius Khan Sauce Pot until chicken is coated. Add green onion sticks and orange slices to pan and simmer 2 minutes to finish.
❑ Serve over rice.

FOOL PROOF TIP: Deglazing is the act of using a liquid to release the flavorful bits of cooked particles in a sauté or roasting pan. This can be as simple as squeezing a lime, adding some wine, or a more sophistocated sauce. For these sauces I've created simple to make, but complex flavored Sauce Pots you can make in one bowl in the microwave. Suitable for deglazing are Spicy Peanut Tai Sauce p. 4, No Genius Khan p. 44, Slick E-Z Beef Glaze p. 28, Slick E-Z Turkey Gravy p. 38, Rosemary Port Glace p. 53, Red Eye Sauce Pot p. 56, and Merlot Balsamic Drizzle p. 73. Even my professional chef friends agree these are really good!! They're from a microwave? You bet.

No Genius Khan Sauce Pot

1/2 C sherry
3 TB Triple Sec
1 C water
1 TB chicken bouillon granules
3 TB sugar
5 TB corn starch
1/2 C orange juice
1 TB soy sauce
2 TB balsamic vinegar
1 tsp All Purpose Taste Massage

- ❑ Mix ingredients together thoroughly in microwavable bowl. Cook on high for 3 minutes stirring twice.
- ❑ Reserve to deglaze pan in Mandarin Chicken Stir Fry.

Margarita Chicken

4 boneless skinless chicken breasts
1 lime (juiced)
2 tsp tequila
2 tsp Triple Sec
1 TB canola oil
5 tsp Santa Fe Sunset Blend

- ❑ Marinate chicken in lime, tequila and Triple Sec for 20-30 minutes.
- ❑ Preheat oven to 450° and skillet on stove top on high heat.
- ❑ Drain chicken and season with 1 tsp Santa Fe per breast.
- ❑ Add canola oil to skillet and heat until just beginning to smoke. Sprinkle remaining tsp Santa Fe in skillet.
- ❑ Sear chicken on both sides until brown (approx 2 minutes per side)
- ❑ Transfer skillet to oven for approx. 8 minutes until cooked through.
- ❑ To serve place chicken on bed of Spanish Rice (p.36) Top with Black Bean Corn Sauce (p.46)

Tangy Picatta of Turkey Chardonnay

4 (3 oz) cutlets of turkey breast (skinless, pounded very thin)
2 tsp Steak & Burger Rubdown
1 C flour seasoned with 2 TB Steak & Burger
1 TB virgin olive oil
12 oz cooked bay shrimp

- ❑ Season pounded turkey cutlets with Steak & Burger at a rate of ½ tsp per 3 oz portion.
- ❑ Preheat skillet on stove top on high heat. Add olive oil to pan and heat until just beginning to smoke.
- ❑ Dredge turkey in seasoned flour. Pat to remove excess.
- ❑ Sauté cutlets quickly for 30 seconds to 1 minute on each side until cooked through.
- ❑ Place cutlets on warm plates of angel hair pasta and spoon on Au Jus Chardonnay. Garnish with lemon sections and steamed bay shrimp.

Au Jus Chardonnay

1/2 C chicken broth
1/2 C Chardonnay
1 TB onion (finely minced)
5 mushrooms (sauté with 1 tsp All Purpose Taste Massage and 1 tsp olive oil)
1 TB heavy cream
2 TB corn starch
1 tsp unsalted butter
1 tsp parsley (chopped)

- ❑ Mix together ingredients *except butter and parsley* in bowl and microwave on high for 5 minutes, stirring twice.
- ❑ Whisk butter and parsley into sauce until smooth.

Slick E-Z Alfredo Sauce

4 cloves garlic (minced fine) add more if you dare
1 TB+ 2 tsp unsalted butter
1 TB water
1 TB corn starch
8 oz whipping cream
1 bay leaf
1/8 tsp nutmeg
1/2 tsp Steak & Burger Rubdown
3/4 C Parmesan cheese (grated)

❑ Place garlic and 1 TB butter in a bowl. Microwave covered on high for 3 minutes, stirring twice.

❑ Add remaining ingredients *except Parmesan and remaining butter* blending well. Microwave 3 minutes stirring twice.

❑ Add Parmesan and remaining butter, whisking until smooth. Microwave 1 minute more. Thin if needed with a little water. Pasta will have some water so don't thin so much sauce won't cling to pasta. Toss with your favorite pasta.

Black Bean Corn Sauce

1 C black beans (canned, drained and washed)
1 C diced tomatoes (canned, drained)
1 C kernel corn
1 C onion (diced medium)
1 can cream of chicken soup
2 TB Santa Fe Sunset Blend
1/2 C white wine
1/2 C water
1/4 C green onion (chopped fine)
2 TB picante sauce

❑ Place ingredients in microwavable bowl and mix thoroughly.

❑ Microwave on high for 6 minutes stirring 3 times.

❑ Serve over Margarita Chicken or grilled pork chops that are seasoned with Santa Fe Sunset Blend.

1-1-1-350 Chicken and Roast Vegetables

1 whole chicken (2½ -3½ lb fryer)
2 TB Fool Proof seasoning blend (your choice)

☐ Preheat oven to 350°
☐ Rub 1 TB Fool Proof on outside of chicken and 1 TB Fool Proof on inside of chicken.
☐ Place in roasting pan.

1 TB olive oil
1 TB All Purpose Taste Massage
3 potatoes (wedge cut in 8ths)
2 onions (wedge cut in 8ths)
4 carrots (rough cut ½" in size)
4 stalks celery (rough cut ½" in size)
8 mushrooms (large, cut in half)

☐ Place oil, All Purpose and vegetables in a bowl. Toss to coat vegetables. Place in a separate roasting pan from chicken.
☐ Roast chicken and vegetables for 1 hour at 350° Cooking time for chicken alone is 1 hour so why not throw in the vegetables. What kinda fool are you?

FOOLISH NOTES: Brush chicken with juices from bottom of pan to insure moist product. For Slick E-Z Gravy follow recipe with turkey dinner (p.38) or Buttermilk Country Gravy (p.30)

FOOL PROOF TIP: Any time you cook meat it is necessary to remove it from the pan and let it rest on a plate or serving platter afterward to let the meat retain its juices. The amount of time depends upon the size of the product. A roast, for example, requires 20 minutes. A roast chicken needs 10 minutes. A single serving size steak or chop, 3 minutes, and so on. Regarding the subject of juiciness, use tongs not a fork to handle meats. Piercing with a fork allows juices to run out. Finally, when slicing product cutting across the grain maximizes tenderness.

Monterey Chicken
With Mango Pepper Salsa

4 boneless skinless chicken breasts
1 lime (juiced)
1 TB + 1 tsp Santa Fe Sunset Blend
2 tsp olive oil
1/4 C red bell pepper (diced)
1/4 C green bell pepper (diced)
1 tsp rice vinegar
2 TB + 2 tsp white wine
1 tsp sugar
1 tsp corn starch
1 medium mango (diced)
2 green onions (diced)
1 TB unsalted butter

- Marinate chicken in lime and 1 TB Santa Fe. Let stand, covered, in refrigerator for 2 hours.
- Heat a skillet on high with 1 tsp olive oil until the oil just begins to smoke. Sear breast about 2 minutes each side, reduce heat to medium and continue cooking about 8-10 minutes. Remove chicken.
- To same skillet add peppers, vinegar, white wine and sugar. Cook until almost tender.
- In a small bowl dissolve cornstarch in remaining 1 tsp white wine. Add mixture to skillet to thicken.
- Add mango, green onion, remaining 1 tsp Santa Fe and butter over low heat until butter is melted and smooth.
- Pour over chicken and serve.

FOOL PROOF TIP: Searing meats first gives them more flavor and locks in juices. Searing over a grill adds yet another dimension of flavor. Taking the time to incorporate these Fool Proof Tips into your cooking techniques will elevate your cooking to the level of professionals.

Stoutly Grilled Guiness Chicken

2 chicken fryers (cut into 8ths for grilling)
1 (16 oz) bottle Guiness Stout Beer
1/2 C ketchup
4 TB All Purpose Taste Massage
1/2 C lt. brown sugar
1/4 C red wine vinegar

❑ In microwavable bowl mix beer, ketchup, 2 TB All Purpose, sugar and vinegar. Microwave 10 minutes on high, stirring twice. Let marinade cool to room temperature.

❑ Marinate chicken in beer mixture for 2 hours massaging about every 30 minutes.

❑ Remove chicken from marinade and sprinkle with remaining 2 TB All Purpose.

❑ Grill chicken beginning skin side down over medium coals for 3-5 minutes. Then turn and finish over medium low heat to insure against burning or charring, about 35-40 minutes. Baste chicken throughout cooking process with Lager's Irish Baster for a super tasty finishing glaze to chicken.

Parmesan Chive Butter Topper

1/4 lb butter or margarine
1/4 C Parmesan cheese
1 tsp granulated garlic
1 tsp All Purpose Taste Massage
1 TB chives (chopped) or green onion chopped very fine
1 tsp white wine

❑ Soften butter. Mix all together well.
❑ On wax paper form into a roll. Twist paper closed to store in refrigerator. Freezes well so make plenty.

THE FOOL SUGGESTS: Use on pasta, baked potato, fantastic garlic bread, on top of fish, poultry, and steak. Put a pat in center of hamburger patty before cooking.

Lager's Irish Baster
Dog Gone Good

1 (16 oz) bottle Guiness Stout Beer
1/4 onion (diced)
4 cloves garlic (diced medium)
1/2 C olive oil
1/2 C lt. brown sugar
1/2 C ketchup
1 TB All Purpose Taste Massage
1 C rice vinegar
2 TB corn starch
1 TB black pepper

❑ In medium hot skillet, sauté onion and garlic in olive oil until caramelized to a rich brown color.
❑ Mix all other ingredients thoroughly in a bowl.
❑ Add to skillet, stir and bring to a boil until thickened and beer no longer produces a foam.
❑ Transfer Baster to blender to emulsify and purée onion and garlic.

FOOLISH NOTE: Lager's Irish Baster is great on products in a smoker and leftover Baster keeps well in refrigerator.

Baked Potato

4 Idaho potatoes
2 TB Steak & Burger Rubdown
2 tsp cooking oil

❑ Rub oil on potatoes. Sprinkle with Steak & Burger.
❑ Roast in preheated 400° oven for 50-60 minutes.
❑ For a really flakey potato, when done poke fork into potato across the top in a cross shape. Place fingers and thumbs at ends of potato, push to pop open the top. It makes the texture and look of potato extra good, no foolin'.

Garlic Martini Grilled Chicken

4 boneless skinless chicken breasts
1/4 C vodka
1/4 C vermouth
3 tsp Steak & Burger Rubdown
1 TB virgin olive oil
2 TB lt. brown sugar
6 cloves garlic (minced)
1 lemon (juiced & zested)

- ❑ Mix all ingredients *except chicken* and microwave on high for 2 minutes.
- ❑ Place chicken in marinade for 30 minutes to 1 hour.
- ❑ Remove and season each breast with ½ tsp Steak & Burger.
- ❑ Cook chicken on hot grill until done through, 8-10 minutes per side.
- ❑ Serve topped with Martini Olive Salad.

Yummo Baked Beans

1/4 lb bacon (diced)
1/2 C onion (diced)
1/2 C green bell pepper
1/2 C lt. brown sugar
2 tsp All Purpose Taste Massage
1/2 C ketchup
1 TB prepared mustard
1 can (28 oz) baked beans (I prefer Bush's)
2 tsp Worcestershire Sauce

- ❑ Preheat skillet on stove top over medium heat.
- ❑ Add bacon, sauté until browned.
- ❑ Add onion and pepper. Sauté until tender.
- ❑ Add sugar and All Purpose cooking 3 minutes.
- ❑ Add remaining ingredients. Bring to a boil then reduce heat to simmer for 1 hour stirring pot occasionally.

Martini Olive Salad

1/2 C stuffed Spanish Queen olives (sliced)
1/2 C cauliflower (coarsely chopped)
1/4 C onion (minced)
1/4 C green bell pepper (diced)
1/4 C red bell pepper (diced)
1/4 C yellow bell pepper (diced)
2 TB parsley (chopped)
1/4 C Parmesan cheese (grated)
1/4 C green onion (diced)
2 TB olive oil
4 TB red wine vinegar
2 TB vermouth
2 TB vodka
1 TB garlic (minced)
3 TB powdered sugar
1 TB Steak & Burger Rubdown

❑ Combine all ingredients in large bowl. Refrigerate to chill before serving.

THE FOOL SUGGESTS: Martini Olive Salad is a great topping for salads and cold cut sandwiches.

FOOLISH NOTE: Try this recipe with grilled cauliflower for an interesting taste treat. Grilling or roasting a few of your ingredients adds an extra dimension of flavor to your favorite recipes. For instance, a light summer marinated vegetable salad gains character from the addition of a grilled onion or roasted corn from the cob. Try roasting your garlic cloves in the toaster oven before mincing into a recipe. Any time you're grilling, include some extra peppers, garlic, onion, whatever, and store in the refrigerator to have on hand. You will be pleased how it enlivens many dishes.

Lamb Chops Dijonnaise
With Rosemary Port Glace

8 lamb chops (center cut 4 oz each)
1/4 C olive oil
1 TB + 2 tsp Steak & Burger Rubdown
1 C bread crumbs
3 eggs (lightly beaten)
1/4 C Dijon mustard

- ❑ Preheat skillet on stove top on medium heat, and oven to 450°
- ❑ Rub lamb chops with 1 TB Steak & Burger.
- ❑ In a bowl, mix remaining 2 tsp Steak & Burger with bread crumbs.
- ❑ In another bowl mix eggs and Dijon, blending well.
- ❑ Bread seasoned chops by first coating thoroughly with egg-mustard mixture, then dredging in seasoned crumbs, patting to make finish smooth.
- ❑ In a preheated skillet, sauté chops in 2 TB olive oil, cooking to a golden brown on each side, about 2 minutes per side, adding olive oil as needed to prevent chops from sticking.
- ❑ Finish cooking in 450° oven. It usually takes another 4-6 minutes in the oven for medium rare.
- ❑ Remove from oven. Serve with Rosemary Port Glace.

Rosemary Port Glace

1/4 C sugar
1/4 C red wine vinegar
1/2 C Ruby Port wine
1/2 C water
1 pkg Knorr Swiss Demi Glace Mix
2 TB shallots
1/2 tsp Steak & Burger Rubdown
1 tsp rosemary (fresh, crushed)
2 tsp unsalted butter

- Mix sugar and vinegar in microwavable bowl. Cook on high 6-7 minutes until vinegar smell disappears and mixture is light brown in color.
- Add port wine, water, shallots, Steak & Burger, Demi Glace Mix. Mix well. Microwave 5 minutes stirring three times.
- Add rosemary. Microwave 1 minute to steep flavor.
- Add butter, whisking until sauce is smooth.

Paillard of Veal Sydney
Elegant Cookout Fare

2 lb veal cutlets (pounded thin)
4 tsp Steak & Burger Rubdown
2 TB extra virgin olive oil
8 oz Gruyere Swiss cheese (sliced thin)
1 avocado (sliced)
6 pats of Parmesan Chive Butter Topper (p.49)
1/2 C Merlot Balsamic Drizzle (p.73)

- Preheat charcoal grill. Preheat oven to 300°
- Rub cutlets with olive oil, sprinkle with Steak & Burger.
- Place cutlets on very hot part of grill for 1-2 minutes each side turning just once.
- Remove from grill. Assemble on ovenproof plates alternating veal, cheese and avocado slices topping with pat of Parmesan Chive Butter
- Place plates in oven for 3-5 minutes until cheese and butter is melted.
- Sauce plates with accents of Merlot Balsamic Drizzle.

FOOL PROOF TIP: Preheating the skillet is mentioned often in this book and for a very good reason. This is possibly my number one tip to you. First, products stick when put on a cold pan. A hot skillet sears the meat locking in the juices. It also creates the brown color finish chefs call carmelization, that gives the product a robust flavor. So take the time and remember, if you will preheat, it will be good to eat!

Roast Loin of Pork
With Apple Mango Stuffing

1 TB olive oil
1 pork loin (approx 4 lb)
4 TB All Purpose Taste Massage
1/2 C bacon (diced)
1/2 C onion (diced medium)
1/2 C celery (diced medium)
1 TB garlic (chopped)
1½ C apple (peeled, diced medium)
1½ C mango (diced medium) mango from a jar okay
1/2 C sherry
2 tsp chicken bouillon granules
4 C bread (white, cubed)
1/2 C mayonnaise
2 egg yolks

❑ Preheat oven to 350°. Preheat skillet on stove top over medium heat.
❑ Split pork loin lengthwise being careful not to split through. Open pork loin flat, wrap in plastic. Pound to flatten slightly. Rub loin with 3 TB All Purpose.
❑ Sear pork loin on all sides in large skillet with olive oil. Remove to platter.
❑ Return skillet to stove, add bacon. Cook until browned, cooked and absent of raw fat.
❑ Add onion, celery, garlic. Sauté until tender, about 3 minutes.
❑ Add apples and mango. Sauté 2 minutes.
❑ Add remaining 1 TB All Purpose, sherry, bouillon and bread cubes. Sauté 3 minutes until bread absorbs liquid.
❑ Remove from stove. Place in bowl. Add egg and mayonnaise. Mix until smooth.
❑ Place pork loin flat on aluminum foil. Place stuffing mix on pork roll. Roll up pork loin in the foil so that stuffing is in middle of pork roll and twist the ends of foil closed. Bake pork roast for 50-60 minutes until internal temperature is 160°

Rudy's Red Eye Baked Ham

10 lb ham (bone in, fully cooked)
2 TB All Purpose Taste Massage
2 cups lt. brown sugar (firmly packed)
3 TB ketchup
1/2 C prepared mustard
2 TB instant coffee granules
1 TB rum extract
Red Eye Sauce Pot

- ❑ Preheat oven to 250°
- ❑ Cut fat cap and white fat layers from ham.
- ❑ Mix all other ingredients and coat ham with glaze.
- ❑ Roast in 250° oven until internal temperature is 140°, about 2½ hours, basting with glaze every 30 minutes.
- ❑ Remove ham from baking pan and place pan on stove top over medium heat. Deglaze with Red Eye Sauce Pot whisking brown bits into gravy. Serve over sliced ham.

Red Eye Sauce Pot

1 TB beef bouillon
1 C red wine
1 C water
1 tsp red wine vinegar
2 TB corn starch

- ❑ Mix all ingredients together thoroughly.

Quick Salad Dressing

1/2 C oil of your choice
1/4 C vinegar
2 TB water
1-2 tsp Fool Proof seasoning of you choice

Hard Seared Pork

2 pork tenderloins (approx 3 lb)
2 TB Steak & Burger Rubdown
1 TB olive oil

- ❑ Preheat skillet on stove top at high heat and oven to 350°
- ❑ Rub pork tenderloin with Steak & Burger.
- ❑ Add olive oil to skillet. Heat until just beginning to smoke.
- ❑ Add tenderloins to pan. Sear well on all sides. Place in 350° oven for 20-25 minutes.
- ❑ Remove from oven and reserve to a platter to capture juices.

Slick E-Z Merlot Butter

1/3 C shallots
2 tsp olive oil
1/2 C Merlot wine
1/2 C water
1 TB beef bouillon granules
2 tsp corn starch
1 TB unsalted butter

- ❑ In a bowl combine shallots and olive oil. Microwave on high 2 minutes.
- ❑ Add Merlot, water, bouillon and corn starch. Mix well. Microwave another 6 minutes stirring twice.
- ❑ Whisk butter into sauce until smooth.

Rosie's Apple Raisin Compote

6 apples (peeled, sliced)
1 TB olive oil
3 TB lt. brown sugar
1/4 C raisins
1/8 tsp cinnamon (powder)
1/8 tsp nutmeg (grated)
1/8 tsp ginger (powdered)

- ❑ Preheat large skillet on stove top over high heat.
- ❑ Add olive oil and heat until just beginning to smoke.
- ❑ Add apples, sauté to brown, approx. 3 minutes.
- ❑ Add raisins, sugar, cinnamon, nutmeg and ginger. Sauté until apples are tender and raisins plump, approx. 2 minutes.

THE FOOL SUGGESTS: On a plate, make a bed of compote, place sliced pork on top and sauce with Slick E-Z Merlot Butter. Yummo!

Hord Ranch Grilled Quail
Sportsman's Treat from the West Texas Cactus Patch

12 blue quail (or other quail or game bird)
1/4 C extra virgin olive oil
3 TB Santa Fe Sunset Blend
1 bunch cilantro (fresh, chopped)
1/2 jalapeño (chopped fine)

- ❑ Clean birds of all feather, etc. immediately to prevent strong game taste.
- ❑ In oil with 2 TB Santa Fe, cilantro and jalapeño, marinate quail overnight.
- ❑ Remove quail from marinade, season with 1 TB Santa Fe.
- ❑ Make ready a grill fire with your favorite wood. On the Hord Ranch mesquite is abundant.
- ❑ Grill quail over high heat for 10-12 minutes turning often to sear all areas of quail.

FOOLISH NOTE: The Fool Proof Baster (p.1) is a great enhancement. Brush on periodically during the grilling process.

John Meyer, President
The Art of Catering
Dallas, Tx.

Grilled Veal Chops with Caponata Relish

4 (12 oz) veal chops
4 tsp Steak & Burger Rubdown
1 TB garlic (crushed)
1/2 tsp rosemary (fresh, chopped)

- ❑ In a small bowl, mix Steak & Burger, garlic and rosemary.
- ❑ Rub into veal chops. Let sit at room temperature to marinate for 2 hours.
- ❑ Prepare grill for cooking.
- ❑ Place chops on the very hot part of the grill searing both sides to lock in juices. Move to cooler area, for approximately 4 minutes per side. Veal chops are best cooked to medium rare.
- ❑ Serve with generous portion of Caponata Relish.

Caponata Relish

1/2 C olive oil
4 tomatoes (peeled, seeded, and chopped)
1/2 onion (minced)
1 TB garlic (minced)
1 pinch dried basil
1 pinch dried oregano
2 tsp All Purpose Taste Massage
1 eggplant (peeled, chopped fine)
5 stalks celery (chopped fine)
1 C green olives (drained, pitted, chopped fine)
1 C pine nuts (toasted)
1/3 C red wine vinegar
1/3 C sugar
1/3 C water
4 TB salt

- ❑ Preheat skillet on stove top on high heat.
- ❑ Add ¼ C olive oil and heat until just beginning to smoke.
- ❑ Add tomatoes, onion, garlic, herbs and 1 tsp All Purpose. Reduce heat and simmer 15 minutes. Remove from heat and set aside.
- ❑ Sprinkle egg plant with salt, toss and let stand at room temperature 20 minutes (removes bitterness in eggplants)
- ❑ In a small pot of boiling water blanch celery and olives. Remove and cool under running water. Pat dry. Mix into tomato mixture.
- ❑ Rinse salt off of eggplant under running water. Drain on paper towels.
- ❑ Heat ¼ C olive oil to almost smoking.
- ❑ Add eggplant, season with All Purpose and sauté for 2 minutes until tender. Add pine nuts and set aside to cool.
- ❑ Add cooled eggplant to tomato mixture.
- ❑ In a small sauce pan heat vinegar, sugar and water cooking for 3 minutes until sugar is dissolved. Remove from heat and set aside to cool.
- ❑ Stir cooled sugar mixture into the Caponata until thick relish consistency is reached. Adjust seasoning with All Purpose to taste.

Kevin Graham, Executive Chef
Las Vegas, Nv.

FOOLISH NOTE: Relish is great with all grilled meats and, believe it or not, angel hair pasta.

FOOL PROOF TIP: Quick E-Z vegetable idea. Wash and chop assorted vegetables. Place in microwavable dish (no need to add water, the water that clings is enough) Microwave covered on high at 2 minute intervals (time will depend on quantity of vegetables and how crispy you like them) When done toss with any of our flavored butters. Zesty Butter for Any Occasion (p.42) Parmesan Chive Butter Topper (p.49) Slick E-Z Merlot Butter (p.57) or Three Citrus Butter (p.69)

Golden Potato Casserole

4 large potatoes (try Yukon Golds) peeling optional
4 TB unsalted butter
1/2 C onion (minced)
1 TB All Purpose Taste Massage
2 C sharp cheddar cheese
2 C sour cream

- ❑ Preheat oven to 350°
- ❑ Boil potatoes whole until cooked through. Remove from water and refrigerate to cool.
- ❑ When potatoes are cold, grate with a hand grater.
- ❑ In medium saucepan over low heat, sweat onions in butter with All Purpose. Add cheese cooking until melted.
- ❑ Add sour cream and blend slightly.
- ❑ Add contents of saucepan to potatoes, mixing well.
- ❑ Pour potato mixture into buttered casserole.
- ❑ Bake in 350° oven for 45 minutes.

Erin T Bell
The Firstborn, just like The Fool
Conroe, Tx.

Buttermilk Chive Dressing

1/4 C buttermilk
1 C mayonnaise
2 TB extra virgin olive oil
1/4 tsp lemon zest
1 TB lemon juice
1 tsp granulated garlic
1 tsp chives (fresh, chopped)
1 TB powdered sugar
1 TB rice vinegar (may substitute white)
1/2 tsp black pepper (fresh ground)
1 TB water

- ❑ Mix in shaker jar. Keep refrigerated.

Carolina Brunswick Crock Roast

6 lb Boston butt pork roast (trimmed of excess fat)
2 tsp olive oil
2 TB All Purpose Taste Massage
2 onions (medium diced)
3/4 C flour
3 TB chicken bouillon granules
1 can (14.5 oz) diced tomatoes with juice
1 C vermouth
3 C water
1/2 C green bell pepper (medium diced)
1/2 C red bell pepper (medium diced)
1 C kernel corn
2 TB apple cider vinegar

❑ Heat crock pot on high setting with olive oil.
❑ Rub trimmed roast with All Purpose. Sear pork roast well in crock pot turning to sear on all sides.
❑ Add onions on top of roast cooking until onions are tender.
❑ In mixing bowl combine flour, bouillon, tomatoes, vermouth and water blending thoroughly making sure no lumps of flour remain.
❑ Pour liquid ingredients into crock pot over roast. Bring to a boil on high for 1 hour.
❑ Reduce to low for 6 hours, until roast is tender and flakes apart with a fork. Skim grease off the stew.
❑ When roast is tender add peppers, corn and vinegar, cooking for an additional hour.

THE FOOL SUGGESTS: Serve in bowls with cornbread.

FOOLISH NOTE: In all of the recipes I suggest a particular Fool Proof seasoning blend. Try them because I do have my reasons for the recommendation, but certainly you can substitute another Fool Proof flavor if you'd like.

Country Style Smothered Pork Chops

3 lb pork chops (thin cut country style)
1 TB Steak & Burger Rubdown
1 C flour seasoned with 2 TB Steak & Burger Rubdown
3 TB olive oil
1/3 C onion (diced)
1/3 C dry sherry
1 can Golden Mushroom Soup
1/4 tsp nutmeg (ground)
4 TB sour cream
1/2 C mushrooms (sautéed)

- Preheat large skillet on stove top over medium high heat.
- Rub chops with Steak & Burger.
- Dredge chops in seasoned flour.
- Sauté in 2 TB olive oil browning on both sides. Remove chops from pan, reserve and keep warm.
- Return skillet to stove. Add onion. Sauté in remaining olive oil for 1-2 minutes browning onion.
- Add sherry, reduce by half.
- Add soup and nutmeg. Bring to a boil.
- Return chops to skillet. Simmer 2-4 minutes until chops are fully cooked and warmed through.
- Remove chops from pan, placing on dinner plates. Whisk sour cream and butter into skillet until smooth. Pour over chops.

THE FOOL SUGGESTS: Serve with rice or mashed potatoes.

FOOLISH NOTE: Since I was a kid I've used cast iron cookware because Mom did. As a professional chef, I continue to use it because I like how it performs. Cast iron transfers heat quickly and evenly. It allows transfer from stove to the oven with great results. The taste transfer is magnificent. I know it's a little work at first to season but it's only a few minutes over a lifetime, they last that long. And it doesn't hurt that cast iron is very affordable.

Tidewater Down East BBQ

7 lb pork butt
7 TB All Purpose Taste Massage

❑ Rub pork butt with All Purpose, cover and store in refrigerator 6 hours to marinate. Do not trim fat for optimum juiciness.

Down East BBQ Baster

1/2 C apple cider vinegar
1/2 C vermouth
1/4 C molasses
1 TB All Purpose Taste Massage
1 tsp liquid smoke
1 TB soy sauce

❑ Prepare charcoal grill and smoker. Sear seasoned butt on all sides over hot grill. Transfer to smoker for the duration of the cooking process (smoking with hickory is traditional).
❑ In a bowl mix the BBQ Baster ingredients thoroughly.
❑ Brush the Baster approximately every 30 minutes while the butt cooks for the next 8-10 hours.
❑ To serve, chop meat and moisten with Carolina BBQ Sauce.

Slick E-Z Oven Version: Transfer pork butt from grill to roasting pan and place in 250° oven. Cook while basting approx. every 30 minutes for 8-10 hours.

Carolina BBQ Sauce

2 C apple cider vinegar
1/8 C sugar
1/8 C All Purpose Taste Massage
1 tsp red pepper flakes

❑ Mix ingredients well in shake bottle.

Ken Presson
Clayton, N.C.

> *THE CAROLINA FOOL SAYS:*
> "Not just Fool Proof
> but fool proven!"

Fillet of Snapper Almondine

4 boneless skinless fillets of Red Snapper can substitute any
2 tsp Steak & Burger Rubdown   white fish
4 TB canola oil
1/2 C flour seasoned with 1 TB Steak & Burger Rubdown
1 lemon (juiced)
2/3 C blanched almonds (sliced)
1 TB unsalted butter
1 TB parsley (fresh, chopped fine)

❑ Preheat skillet on stove top over medium heat. Season fillets with Steak & Burger.

❑ Dredge snapper in seasoned flour. Pat dry to remove excess flour.

❑ Add canola oil to skillet and allow 2-3 minutes for oil to heat in pan. Place snapper in pan skin side up *the skin side is flatter due to the knife action used to remove skin.*

❑ Sauté for approximately 3-4 minutes on each side *cooking times for fish are approximate at best because the thickness varies even within the same fillet, so never leave fish on the burner unattended because the only true indication for sautéed fish is a golden brown color and flaky texture.*

❑ Remove fish when done and place on warm plates. Pour lemon juice evenly over sautéed fillets.

❑ Wipe pan lightly to remove excess grease and brown bits and return pan to stove.

❑ Add butter and almonds to pan over medium heat stirring to prevent scorching for about 2-3 minutes. *Again don't leave the pan...watch it. No foolin!*

❑ When almonds are golden brown butter should be at a bubbly stage and pan will emit a sweet nutty aroma.

❑ Add chopped parsley and immediately spoon almond/butter mixture over fish and serve post haste.

Smokey Flavor Crispy Fish
A Ten Dollar Name for a Slick E-Z Dish

4 (6-7 oz) fish fillets (deboned, skinned)
5 tsp Steak & Burger Rubdown
2 tsp olive oil
1 lemon (cut in half)

❑ Preheat cast iron skillet on stove on high heat and turn the kitchen fan on high while you're at it.
❑ Season fillets with Steak & Burger Rubdown at a rate of 1 tsp per fillet.
❑ Add olive oil to very hot pan, heat until just beginning to smoke. Then sprinkle remaining Steak & Burger on hot pan. Immediately place fish in pan skin side up.
❑ Char both sides of fish 3-5 minutes per side until it flakes to the touch.
❑ Just before removing from pan squeeze the lemon onto fish.

Slick E-Z Version: Cook as above in a very hot skillet with smoking oil, searing skin side of fish for two minutes. Turn fish, cover and remove pan from heat and leave covered 4-6 minutes, depending how done you like your fish. Squeeze lemon in pan. You're done!

Slick E-Z Rémoulade

1 TB onion (minced)
1 tsp caper (minced)
2 tsp pickle relish
1/2 tsp parsley (chopped)
1/4 tsp Seafood Serenade
1/4 C mayonnaise
1/2 tsp Dijon mustard
3 drops Tabasco

❑ Mix ingredients well in bowl.

Ty's Salmon Fantasy

1 side of salmon (deboned and skinned)
2 cloves garlic
1 oz basil (fresh, chopped)
1 oz dill (fresh, chopped)
1 bulb shallots (puréed)
8 oz lump crabmeat (picked clean)
6 oz lobster meat (puréed raw)
3 oz heavy cream
2 TB Seafood Serenade
2 eggs (slightly beaten)
2 oz brandy
2 oz spinach (cleaned, picked)
1 sheet of puff pastry (12" x 12")

❑ To prepare lobster-crab mousse:
In a food processor purée garlic, herbs, shallots, lobster, crabmeat, cream, 1 TB Seafood Serenade and 1 egg. Slowly add brandy to mixture being careful to maintain the thickness of mousse. (Note: it may not take all of the brandy in which case the chef may have to dispose of the extra in any way he sees fit) *It is necessary that the mousse be thick.*

❑ In a large bowl fold the spinach leaves into the mousse and refrigerate for 3 hours to set up.

❑ Slice salmon lengthwise in half being careful not to go through to the other side. Place the butterflied salmon in plastic wrap and pound evenly flat to approximately 1/4" – 3/8" thickness. (If you ask your local butcher nicely, he could do this for you)

❑ Preheat oven to 325°

❑ On a large floured surface roll out your defrosted puff pastry to 2" larger on all sides than the salmon fillet.

❑ Place the pounded salmon fillet edge to edge next to your pastry. Spread the lobster-crab mousse on top of fish entirely covering the fillet. Slowly roll salmon toward pastry sheet jelly-roll style until totally rolled up and at edge of pastry.

❑ Season salmon roll with remaining 1 TB of Seafood Serenade.

- Continue rolling salmon forward onto pastry, rolling to wrap salmon in pastry. Close pastry edge together using some of remaining beaten egg as a wash to seal.
- Carefully place salmon roll on a parchment paper lined baking pan.
- Egg wash entire pastry with remaining egg to make pastry golden brown.
- Bake for 35-40 until pastry is golden brown on all sides.
- Serve within 15 minutes after removing from oven. Slice with a bread knife or electric knife for best presentation. Serve with Tangy Caper Cream.

Ty Thoren, Executive Chef
Renaissance Hotel
Dallas, Tx.

Tangy Caper Cream

1/4 C chicken broth
1/4 C white wine
3 TB shallots (minced fine)
2 TB corn starch
1 TB capers (chopped)
1/4 tsp nutmeg
1/4 tsp Steak & Burger Rubdown
1/4 C sour cream
1 tsp green onion (chopped)
1 tsp parsley (chopped)
1 tsp unsalted butter

- In a microwavable bowl, mix chicken broth, wine, shallots and corn starch.
- Microwave on high for 4 minutes stirring 3 times.
- Whisk in capers, nutmeg, Steak & Burger, and sour cream. Return to microwave another minute.
- Whisk green onion, parsley and butter until butter melts and is smooth.

Sara's Crusty Marinated Salmon

1 lb salmon fillets (deboned & skinned)
1/2 lemon (juiced)
1/4 C Italian dressing *The Fool* prefers Newman's
4 TB Seafood Serenade
4 TB all purpose flour
1/2 tsp black pepper (to taste) optional
1/4 C olive oil

❑ Cut salmon on the bias into ½" strips. In a bowl, marinate salmon slices in lemon juice and Italian dressing for 5 minutes.
❑ Mix Seafood Serenade, flour and pepper in a separate bowl.
❑ Remove fish from marinade and dredge in flour mixture patting to remove excess.
❑ Add olive oil to hot skillet and heat until just beginning to smoke. Add breaded salmon to skillet cooking quickly, approx. 2 minutes per side, almost blackening the fish.
❑ Remove and drain on paper towels.

Three Citrus Butter

1/2 orange (juiced)
1 lemon (juiced)
1 lime (juiced)
2 TB Chardonnay wine
1/2 tsp Seafood Serenade
1 tsp corn starch
2 tsp water
2 TB unsalted butter

❑ Mix all ingredients *except butter* in a microwavable bowl. Cook on high for 6-8 minutes stirring twice. Whisk butter into sauce until melted and smooth. Spoon over Sara's Salmon, or any fish, chicken or steak.

Sara Pierce, age 11
Troy, Mi.

The Seafood Gourmet's Sure Fire Grill

4 (6 oz) fillets of sea bass
2 tsp Seafood Serenade
2 oz soy sauce
1 oz tequila
4 cloves garlic (minced)
1 tsp fresh ginger (grated)

❑ Combine soy sauce, tequila, garlic and ginger in a bowl. Pour mixture over fish fillets, marinate for 20 minutes.
❑ Remove fish from marinade and sprinkle both sides of fish with Seafood Serenade at a rate of ½ tsp per fillet.
❑ Place fish immediately on very hot grill for 4-6 minutes turning once. (Oil grill grate to prevent fish from sticking)

Chef Didier Busnot
The Seafood Gourmet Market
Jacksonville, Fl.

FOOLISH NOTE: This recipe is from Chef Didier Busnot, affectionately known to his customers as *The Seafood Gourmet* and feared by fish the world over! When you're in Jacksonville you can buy the *best* fish from him at his market.

FOOL PROOF TIP: This marinade and cooking technique works well for any fish.

Crazy Like a Roasted Nut

2 C any nuts (raw, unsalted)
2 TB favorite Fool Proof flavor
2 tsp oil of your choice

❑ Preheat oven to 350° Place nuts on baking sheet in single layer. Roast 15-18 minutes.
❑ Toss nuts together with oil and Fool Proof. Let cool.

Eat 'em up. Toss 'em on salad. Top a fish or chicken. Any time a recipe calls for nuts this roasted nut will give greater flavor.

Matt Daddy's Killer Crab Supremes

1/3 C onion (diced small)
2 ¼ C green bell pepper (diced small)
1/3 C celery (diced small)
1 C + 2 TB unsalted butter
1 tsp garlic (minced)
1/4 C flour
1 ¼ C milk (warmed for 30 seconds in microwave)
1 tsp Steak & Burger Rubdown
1 TB Seafood Serenade
1 tsp Worcestershire Sauce
1 TB Dijon mustard
2 TB Parmesan cheese (grated)
2/3 C sharp cheddar cheese (grated)
1 jar (4.5 oz) mushrooms (sliced, drained)
2 lb lump crabmeat (picked clean of any shell)
1 C Ritz cracker crumbs (mixed with 1 tsp paprika)
8 individual terrines (buttered)

❑ Preheat oven to 325°. Also preheat large deep skillet on stove top over medium heat.
❑ In skillet sauté onion, pepper, celery in 2 tsp butter until tender.
❑ Add garlic and continue sautéing until vegetables begin to brown slightly (approx. 3 minutes). Remove vegetables from pan and reserve. Return pan to heat.
❑ Melt remaining butter then whisk in flour. Continue whisking roux for approx. 3 minutes until smooth and bubbly but not browned.
❑ Add warm milk slowly, whisking constantly until smooth.
❑ Reduce heat to low. Simmer 10-15 minutes until flour taste has gone from sauce. *Do not boil or scorch.*
❑ Add Steak & Burger, Seafood Serenade, Worcestershire, Dijon, Parmesan and cheddar. Whisk while simmering 3-5 minutes until mixture is the consistency of pancake batter.
❑ Add mushrooms, sautéed vegetables and crab meat. Mix well

for 1-2 minutes. Remove from heat.

❑ Place crab mixture into buttered terrines. Bake for 20 minutes at 325°

❑ Remove from oven. Top with cracker crumb mixture. Return to oven 3-5 minutes until browned on top and crab mix is bubbly.

FOOLISH NOTE: Supremes may be made ahead that morning or the day before. Bring Supremes to room temperature before baking.

Matt Pierce
Matt Daddy's Hunt & Fish Camp
Clarkston, Mi.

Grilled Vegetable Bobs

1 bell pepper (cut in large pieces)
1 zucchini (wedged in 8 pieces)
1 yellow squash (wedged in 8 pieces)
1 tomato (wedged in 8 pieces)
1 red onion (wedged in 8 pieces, microwaved 3 minutes)
4 mushrooms (cut in half)
1/4 C virgin olive oil
1 tsp granulated garlic
1 TB soy sauce
2 TB balsamic vinegar
2 TB All Purpose Taste Massage
2 tsp lt. brown sugar
1 TB Worcestershire Sauce
6-8 wooden skewers (soaked in water)

❑ Assemble vegetables in alternating fashion on skewers.

❑ Mix remaining ingredients and marinate veggie bobs for 30 minutes. Remove from marinade and sprinkle with remaining All Purpose.

❑ Place on hot grill 3-4 minutes per side. Do watch so they don't stick or burn. Brush with marinade to serve.

Bacon Wrapped Prawn Brochettes
With Merlot Balsamic Drizzle

24 large shrimp (cleaned, peeled & deveined)
12 slices bacon (*The Fool* likes mesquite smoked)
4 tsp Seafood Serenade
4 TB spicy brown mustard
4 wooden skewers (soaked in water)

❑ Preheat grill.
❑ Partially cook bacon 4 minutes in microwave on high.
❑ Season peeled shrimp with Seafood Serenade.
❑ Brush one side of par-cooked bacon strips with mustard and cut in two. Wrap each seasoned shrimp with bacon, mustard side toward shrimp.
❑ Skewer 6 wrapped shrimp per brochette. Place shrimp skewers over medium-hot coals for 3-5 minutes each side, turning brochettes from time to time during the cooking process to prevent burning of bacon.

THE FOOL SUGGESTS: Serve over pilaf of Claude's Valencian Rice (p.74) and flavor with Merlot Balsamic Drizzle.

Merlot Balsamic Drizzle

1 slice of bacon (minced)
1 TB sweet onion (minced fine)
1 clove garlic (minced)
1 TB sugar
1/2 C Merlot wine
1 tsp corn starch
1/4 C balsamic vinegar
1/2 tsp Steak & Burger Rubdown
1 TB ketchup

❑ In a bowl microwave bacon until crispy, about 3 minutes.

- In a separate bowl, mix Merlot and corn starch. Add to bacon mixture, whisking well.
- Add remaining ingredients mixing well. Microwave another 5 minutes stirring twice.
- Whisk very well prior to serving. Drizzle over shrimp brochettes.

FOOLISH NOTE: For a less tangy drizzle, reduce vinegar.

THE FOOL SUGGESTS: Merlot Balsamic Drizzle is wonderful over grilled fish, chicken and steak when you don't want a sauce but want additional flavor.

Claude's Valencian Rice

2 TB virgin olive oil
1/2 C smoked ham (diced small)
2 TB garlic (minced fine)
1/3 C onion (diced small)
1/3 C red bell pepper (diced small)
1/3 C green bell pepper (diced small)
1 TB All Purpose Taste Massage
3 C cooked rice (saffron rice is extra good)
1/4 C green onion (minced)

- Preheat large skillet on stove top over medium heat.
- Add olive oil, heat for 1 minute.
- Add ham, garlic, onion, bell peppers and All Purpose in that order and sauté for 3 minutes.
- Add cooked rice and cook 3 minutes to warm through.
- Add green onion stirring into rice mixture for 30 seconds prior to serving.

Roasted Garlic Grilled Grouper

4 (7 oz) grouper fillets (boned, skinned)
4 TB dry vermouth
2 whole bulbs of garlic (cut in half across)
1 tsp olive oil
6 tsp Steak & Burger Rubdown
4 TB unsalted butter
1/4 tsp balsamic vinegar
1 TB chives (fresh, chopped)
1/4 tsp Seafood Serenade

- ❑ Preheat oven to 350° to roast garlic (I use a toaster oven)
- ❑ Marinate grouper in 3 TB + 2 tsp vermouth for 20 minutes.
- ❑ In a small pan place garlic bulb, cut in half. Coat with ½ tsp olive oil and 1 tsp Steak & Burger. Roast 50-60 minutes in 350° oven until roasted soft and golden brown.
- ❑ Remove from oven, squeeze roasted cloves from bulb into food processor. Purée on high.
- ❑ Add ½ tsp olive oil, butter, vinegar, chives, remaining vermouth, 1 tsp Steak & Burger and ¼ tsp Seafood Serenade to garlic. Blend well.
- ❑ Remove fish from vermouth. Season with small amount of garlic butter mixture and 1 tsp Steak & Burger per fillet. Place on hot grill 8-12 minutes (depends on thickness) turning once.
- ❑ Serve grilled fish with roasted garlic butter and fresh lemon.

Spare Parts Rice

2 TB olive oil
1/4 C each onion, celery, green bell pepper (diced medium)
1/2 C leftover meat diced (chicken, pork, beef, seafood)
1/4 C frozen veggies (peas, corn)
1/4 C tomato (diced)
1 C rice (cooked)
1 tsp Steak & Burger Rubdown

- ❑ Over medium heat sauté ingredients in order very quickly. Total cooking time is 2 minutes.

Tom's Matzo-Be Fried Scallops

1 lb scallops (fresh, side muscle removed)
1 C all purpose flour
2 TB Seafood Serenade
1 C matzo meal
1/2 C Italian bread crumbs
1 egg (beaten)
1 TB milk
3-4 C canola oil

- ❏ In home fryer or deep skillet to preheat oil to 350°
- ❏ Drain scallops of liquid and pat dry.
- ❏ Mix flour and Seafood Serenade in one bowl. Mix matzo meal and bread crumbs in another bowl.
- ❏ Beat eggs with milk in third bowl.
- ❏ Coat scallops in flour mixture patting off excess.
- ❏ Transfer to egg mixture a few at a time.
- ❏ Immediately roll scallops in matzo mixture coating well.
- ❏ Fry scallops a few at a time for 3-4 minutes until golden brown. Remove to paper towel to drain. Sprinkle immediately with Seafood Serenade to taste.
- ❏ Serve with fresh lemon wedge and tartar sauce.

FOOLISH NOTE: This recipe was one of those happy accidents. Tom ran out of flour for traditional fried scallops so he substituted matzo meal and it made for a uniquely crunchy product.

Emilio Thomas Valentin, Corporate Executive Chef
Culinaire International Inc.
Miami, Fl.

FOOL PROOF TIP: There are several recipes in this book for seasoned butters. When you're preparing them make plenty because they freeze well. (portion them to serving size pats before freezing so you don't have to defrost the whole stick) Anytime you'd use butter, use these better butters.

Cancun Fish and Sunset Chips
With Chile-Tartar Sauce

6 catfish or cod fillets (6-8 oz portions)
4 TB Santa Fe Sunset Blend
1 TB cilantro (chopped) optional
1 C corn meal
1 C milk
1 C canola oil

- Preheat oil in deep skillet over medium heat.
- Mix 2 TB Santa Fe, cilantro and corn meal in a bowl.
- Place milk in a separate bowl.
- Rub fish filets with 1 TB Santa Fe. Dip fish in milk then dredge through cornmeal mixture patting to remove excess.
- Place fish in hot oil, frying each side for 3-5 minutes until done. Remove cooked fish from oil and drain on paper towel. Immediately sprinkle fish with remaining 1 TB Santa Fe.
- Serve with Sunset Chips, Chile-Tartar Sauce and fresh lime.

Chile-Tartar Sauce

1/2 C mayonnaise
4 tsp Santa Fe Sunset Blend
1/2 tsp jalapeño (minced)
1/4 tsp cilantro
1/4 C sweet pickle relish
1/4 tsp spicy brown mustard
2 tsp green onion (minced)
1 tsp lime (zest)

- Mix ingredients in a bowl thoroughly.
- Chill in refrigerator

Sunset Chips

6 potatoes (skin on, sliced very thin)
2 C canola oil
3 TB Santa Fe Sunset Blend

❑ Preheat large skillet with canola oil over medium high heat to 350°
❑ Cook potatoes in stages being careful not to overload oil. This will ensure maximum browning and crispiness. Fry potatoes approximately 5-6 minutes until golden brown and crispy. Stir and turn potatoes throughout cooking process. When done drain on paper towels. Immediately sprinkle with Santa Fe to your taste.

FOOLISH NOTE: Allow oil to reheat between batches to ensure all your chips are chip like.

White Beans El Dorado

1 slice bacon (minced raw)
1 mediun onion (diced)
2 stalks celery (diced)
1/2 green bell pepper (diced)
1 clove garlic (minced)
1 TB Santa Fe Sunset Blend
1 can (15 oz) white northern beans (drained, rinsed)
1 can (14.5 oz) diced tomatoes in juice
1 bay leaf
1/2 tsp chicken bouillon granules

❑ In a large casserole microwave bacon on high heat 2 minutes until brown. Add onion, celery, pepper, garlic and Santa Fe. Cook for 5 minutes stirring twice.
❑ Add beans, tomatoes with juice, bay leaf and chicken bouillon. Microwave 10 minutes stirring 3 times.

Whacky Cake
The Fool's Chocolate Inspiration

3 C all purpose flour
2 tsp baking soda
2 C sugar
6 TB cocoa
1 tsp salt
2 TB vinegar
12 TB (6 oz) canola oil
2 tsp vanilla
2 C cold water

- ❏ Preheat oven to 350°
- ❏ Sift all dry ingredients into an ungreased 13 x 9" baking pan. Blend well with a fork.
- ❏ With the back of a spoon form three holes in the mixture. Fill one hole with vanilla, one with vinegar and one with oil. Then pour water over all.
- ❏ Use a fork to mix. (Batter may be a bit lumpy but don't worry—this cake is truly Fool Proof)
- ❏ Bake in 350° oven for 40 minutes until toothpick inserted in center comes out clean.

Dorothy Ehrisman
Jacksonville, N.C.

NOT SO FOOLISH TESTIMONIAL: As a boy I would sit at the kitchen table while Mrs. Dorothy baked her wonderful desserts. Her happiness in bringing great tasting treats to her family and friends is one of my fondest memories and inspired me to want to do the same. So my idea to grow up and be a chef was born. My toque is off to you Mrs. Dorothy. Thanks for the inspiration and the recipes.

Peanut Butter Rum Frosting
Mrs. Dorothy likes this frosting on Whacky Cake

1/3 C peanut butter
1½ tsp vanilla
1½ tsp rum extract
1½ tsp butter extract
1/3 C milk
3 C powdered sugar

- ❑ Blend peanut butter and sugar.
- ❑ Stir in vanilla, milk and extracts. Beat until smooth and spreadable. Add more milk or sugar to adjust consistency.

Dorothy Ehrisman
Jacksonville, N.C.

Jack Daniel's Pecan Pie

1 C lt. brown sugar
1/4 C unsalted butter
1/4 tsp salt
1 C dark corn syrup
4 eggs (beaten)
1 tsp vanilla
2 TB + 2 tsp Jack Daniel's bourbon
1 ¼ C pecans (halves & pieces)
1 pie crust shell

- ❑ Preheat oven to 450°
- ❑ Cream butter and sugar together until fluffy.
- ❑ Add salt, corn syrup, eggs, vanilla and bourbon and mix.
- ❑ Line pie shell with pecans and pour in filling.
- ❑ Bake at 450° for 10 minutes.
- ❑ Reduce temperature to 350° and bake another 35 minutes until knife inserted into center comes out clean.

Mrs. Dorothy's Carrot Cake

1½ C canola oil
2 C sugar
3 eggs
2 C flour
2 tsp cinnamon
1 tsp baking soda
1 pkg. (7 oz) coconut
1 C walnuts (chopped)
1 can (15½ oz) crushed pineapple (drained)
2 C carrots (shredded)
2 tsp vanilla

- ❏ Preheat oven to 350°
- ❏ Mix together oil, sugar and eggs.
- ❏ Add sifted dry ingredients. Mix together until well blended.
- ❏ Add coconut, walnuts, pineapple, carrots and vanilla. Mix well.
- ❏ Pour into greased and floured 9 X 13 X 2" baking pan.
- ❏ Bake 50-60 minutes. Cool. Frost with cream cheese frosting.

Cream Cheese Frosting

8 oz cream cheese
1 lb powdered sugar
1 stick unsalted butter
2 tsp vanilla

- ❏ Blend cream cheese and butter well.
- ❏ Add sugar and beat until smooth and fluffy.
- ❏ Add vanilla blending well.

FOOLISH NOTE: Cake freezes well although ours never makes it to the freezer so make two!
Dorothy Ehrisman
Jacksonville, N.C.

Bananas Foster Ice Cream
A New Orleans Favorite in One Scoop

6 egg yolks
10 eggs
1 Qt heavy cream
1 Qt Half & Half
3 C lt. brown sugar
1 TB unsalted butter
1 C sugar
1 tsp cinnamon
1/4 tsp nutmeg
2 TB vanilla
2 tsp banana extract
2 tsp rum extract
4 bananas (very ripe, sliced)
Ice Cream Machine and rock salt

❑ Place eggs and egg yolks together in a large bowl and whip lightly.
❑ Place all other ingredients *except bananas* in a large heavy saucepan and blend well. Place on medium heat stirring often to prevent scorching. Gradually increase heat to medium high while continuing to whip, eventually bringing to a scalding low boil.
❑ Slowly add boiling cream mixture to bowl of eggs while whipping constantly to prevent curdling.
❑ Add sliced bananas to custard mixture blending well.
❑ Chill ice cream mix in refrigerator until very cold.
❑ Turn in ice cream machine according to instructions.
❑ Let finished ice cream harden in freezer 4-6 hours.

Slick E-Z Apple Tart

4-5 apples (peeled, sliced)
1 sheet frozen puff pastry (12" x 12")
2/3 C sugar
1/4 tsp cinnamon
1/4 tsp ginger
1/4 tsp nutmeg
4 TB unsalted butter

- ❑ Defrost puff pastry.
- ❑ Preheat skillet on stove top over medium high heat and oven to 350°
- ❑ Add butter to skillet. Add the apples.
- ❑ Increase heat to high stirring apples constantly for 5 minutes until brown.
- ❑ Add sugar, cinnamon, ginger and nutmeg. Stir and sauté for 1 minute.
- ❑ Place pastry on top of apples in skillet trimming excess to form circle.
- ❑ Place in 350° oven for 20 minutes.
- ❑ Invert skillet after taking tart from oven onto a serving platter.
- ❑ Double yummo with vanilla bean ice cream!

Tiffany's Summer Freeze

12 large strawberries (frozen)
1/2 C powdered sugar
6 scoops frozen vanilla yogurt
1/2 tsp vanilla
3/4 C milk

- ❑ Place all ingredients in a blender.
- ❑ Purée mixture thoroughly.
- ❑ Tiffany says to increase milk for a shake.

Tiffany Keresztenyi, age 12
Manchester, Md.

White Chocolate Bread Pudding

1 lb French bread loaf (toasted: cut in cubes, bake dry @ 350° for 20 minutes)
1/4 tsp nutmeg
1 Qt Half & Half
1 can (14 oz) sweetened condensed milk
1 C sugar
2 TB vanilla
8 TB unsalted butter
10 whole eggs
1 pkg (12 oz) white chocolate chips
1 pkg (6 oz) Craisins from Ocean Spray may substitute
3 tsp cinnamon   regular raisins
4 TB lt. brown sugar

- In a large bowl blend eggs.
- In a large pot mix well Half & Half, nutmeg, condensed milk, sugar, vanilla and 4 TB butter. Bring to a scalding boil. Whisk *very slowly* into beaten eggs. Set aside.
- Divide 4 TB lt. brown sugar and 4 TB butter cut into slivers evenly into two 9" cake pans covering bottoms. Then divide bread cubes into the two pans. Place white chocolate and craisins evenly over top of bread. Finish with cinnamon sprinkled on top.
- Preheat oven to 275°
- Pour custard mixture evenly into the two pans. Press bread down into custard mixture and allow to absorb. Let stand 1 hour pressing again every ten minutes.
- Cover with aluminum foil. Place each pan in larger deep baking pan with 1 inch of water (water bath prevents custard desserts like this from burning in the oven).
- Bake in 275° oven for 2½ to 3 hours. Remove from oven.

FOOLISH NOTE: For a down home version, save all leftover pieces of bread in freezer until you have enough for this pudding. Also leftover chocolate candy of any kind, put it in.

Fool Proof Menus

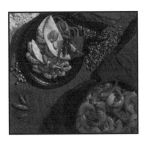